MY CHOSEN WORDS

GREENLAND (DENMARK)
ALASKA (USA)
CANADA
UNITED STATES OF AMERICA
MEXICO
VENEZUELA
COLOMBIA
PERU
BRAZIL
BOLIVIA
ARGENTINA
FRANCE
SPAIN
ALGERIA
MALI

RUSSIA
UKRAINE
KAZAKHSTAN
MONGOLIA
CHINA
JAPAN
TURKEY
SYRIA
IRAQ
IRAN
INDIA
EGYPT
SAUDI ARABIA
SUDAN
ETHIOPIA
SOMALIA
ZAMBIA
THAILAND
MALAYSIA
INDONESIA
AUSTRALIA
NEW ZEALAND

MY CHOSEN WORDS

Memories of a Professional Immigrant Woman

FERIAL IMAM HAQUE

ISBN-13:
978-1-952405-76-1   [Paperback Edition]
978-1-952405-75-4   [eBook Edition]

Printed and bound in The United States of America.

Published by

The Mulberry Books, LLC.
8330 E Quincy Avenue,
Denver CO 80237

themulberrybooks.ctom

In memory of my late mother, the inspirational
Professor Akhtar Imam

and

To my late father,
Professor Ali Imam, and his sweet memory

The woman I was yesterday introduced me to the woman I am today, which makes me very excited about meeting the woman I will become tomorrow.

Introduction

My Chosen Words is a personal narrative of the life of Ferial Imam Haque in her teens. Included are many reflections of her teenage dreams while she was growing up in East Pakistan in the care of her widowed mother.

She is proud of having grown up in a family that practiced traditional Bengali culture and made an educational imprint in the forties, as described in Chapter 1. In Chapter 2 she expresses her personal ideas of who she wanted to be in the global community. Her impressions in subsequent chapters of living in different cities in many countries give the reader a glimpse of other people and their lives.

Then her story of embarking on a new journey in a new country to make her home with her family in the early seventies as an immigrant woman is fascinating. It was a journey of triumph and turmoil, her having left behind the memories of living on the battlefield of East Pakistan.

She adopted a new lifestyle to enjoy each day and celebrate something new in a country of diverse cultures and ideas. Concluding with the stories of her living experiences of the Canadian winter, the beauty of nature, the colorful fall and spring between enjoying the bounty of summer harvest and celebrating it, she shows herself to be a proud Canadian.

Contents

Prelude to Chapter 7

Prelude to Chapter 8

Prelude to Chapter 9

Prelude to Chapter 10

Prelude to Chapter 1

The recollection of the stories of Ferial Imam Haque's life begins at her mother's paternal grandmother's house. These are early memories of growing up under the care of Ferial's widowed mother with her two sisters in the early forties. Many stories and memories are of the echoes she could hear of her relatives and her mother's friends. She and her two sisters were the center of attention in their schools, colleges and universities, and among their family and friends.

Chapter 1

Family

You don't choose your family. They are God's gift to you as you are to them.

—Desmond Tutu

September 21, 2016

Grandfather's House

My childhood memories of Grandfather's house are like fairy tale stories. His house covers the many centuries of many generations of mother's father's family. This is the house where I grew up when Mother, in her twenties, moved after Father's premature death in the early 1940's.

I grew up there, forming the foundation of my formative years. I feel that there is where I was given the building blocks to cope with social rituals and taboos in the forties in British India. Many decades later during the liberation movement of Bangladesh, I took refuge in Grandfather's house with my daughter. Thank you, Grandfather, for keeping this house for the family and for keeping the history of your family alive.

In my culture, we call Grandfather "Nana." Nana will always occupy a soft spot of my heart. He taught me how to write my alphabets—Bengali, English, Arabic and Urdu—with a special feather pen. I was excited to dip the feather pen in the square glass ink pot, making sure there was not too much ink on it, because otherwise it would smudge. Once I finished my writing, the page had to be blotted carefully with white blotting paper. I learned many skillful techniques from Nana.

Later, in the fifties in London, England, at school I always got high marks for calligraphic writing. Even during my research in the field of forensic science, my supervisors and the office staff who typed my reports and research papers to be published complimented me on my handwriting.

I stop to think what a great teacher Nana was. Thank you, Nana! You will always be beside me when I am composing my research findings for publication or composing a story about my childhood, youth, or adulthood. Now in my senior years, sitting in my computer room just to capture my memories to put down in words, I revisit myself sitting beside you each time, and I continue to write with confidence.

I did not have a father figure in my life while growing up, but I always remember how kind you were to accept Mother as a young widow with three little daughters. Cruel social limits were imposed on her. She became misfortunate when father passed away. She had no son, only three daughters, so society looked upon her and us with great pity. Knowing of these limitations for women, I was determined to acquire the highest degree so I could speak with confidence and dream of a better world for women in the global community. My motto in life was "Do or Die." Yes, I succeeded on my promise when I was awarded my doctor of philosophy degree in science by Strathclyde University, Glasgow, Scotland.

When I was in Ottawa, Canada, as a new bride adjusting to the new customs of my husband, I was sometimes bewildered, but I remembered you, Nana, and your wisdom of family tradition. I carefully wiped my tears with a clean handkerchief so nobody would know my heart was breaking with the pain of being in a foreign land. This was in the sixties. I was lost in a long, cold winter in a land covered with white snow.

Like a child, I would forget my sorrows and responsibility of learning to be a wife. I would remind myself I should practice writing my alphabets—Bengali, Urdu, and Arabic—lest I forget them. Last but not least, I studied my Bengali music notes. With so much struggle, I managed to continue with my studies and to practice the skills I learned from Juharon's mother, our housekeeper. She had many unique characteristics. Now I realize she was a women's gender equality spokesperson whose slogan was "We all have equal rights as human beings."

A lesson I learned from her and Mother is that education is the key to a woman's dignity and self-identity, no matter what happens in life. My objective here is not to broadcast the turmoil and stormy days of my life. Yet I wish to write about the life I live each day in peace and harmony as I walk toward the end of my dreams.

Why Am I Different?

Because

I'm a little girl made of sugar and spice
With a sweet smile that's so nice.

My father walked through the gates of heaven
Without telling me.
Now, he is going to sleep forever without pain,

Leaving his three infant daughters, all under five,
With his wise and loving wife.

I thank him for his legacy and his link with
The Bose–Einstein theory.
Father completed his MSc thesis under
Professor S. N. Bose.

Image of Father in his BSc honors convocation gown in 1935 in
front of the Physics Department, Carzen Hall, Dhaka University

FERIAL IMAM HAQUE

I still miss my father and love him,

But

At the thought of loving his mother,
I get the jitters and tears wet my cheeks

Because

She wouldn't send Father for treatment.
He'd have to cross the rough waters of the
Bay of Bengal, the Arabian Sea, the Suez Canal, the Red Sea and the
Atlantic Ocean to go to London, England,
for treatment in the early forties.

In 1950, when I was traveling by ship
With Mother, I thought, *O Grandma!*
Because of your decision, I grew up
Without cherishing Father's love.

Dear Mother, thank you for your love,
Dedication, and sincerity to inspire
Your three daughters to become a
Physician, a chemist, and a physicist,
Following in our parents' footsteps.

This may be your legacy, but I enjoyed
The merit of my knowledge and education
Growing up in a faraway land called
Ottawa, in Ontario, Canada, and living there for five decades.

Today, in my golden years, I keep myself
Active by learning many fields of science and society,
But I never stop to say what a miserable life it is
Alone, managing my day-to-day essentials
Of life and still enjoying my faith in learning.

Why Do I Feel Different?

Because

Ma said goodbye to us on June 22, 2009, forever to
Sleep in peace in her final resting place!

I was bewildered and stood on the highway of confusion.
I had nowhere to go, nobody to turn to.

Ma was my mentor and nurtured me with her wisdom and love.
Her example had a catalytic effect on me all throughout my life.

Without her presence, I lost my direction and my road map for living.
Time is the healer of many wounds, I have discovered.

My memory of Ma having been widowed at age twenty-five
Is a lesson to learn for many women and widows.

Because

She had no son, she became a second-class citizen
Within a fraction of second.

How boldly she faced the cruel rituals of society
To set an example for many women in their widowhood to
Independently live with dignity.

Thank you, Mother, for

Nurturing me with your wisdom, love, care, and knowledge, and
Being so patient while I was growing up without a father.

Ma's dedication and hard work make her a role model
For young women, including her students who are scattered

Worldwide.

FERIAL IMAM HAQUE

Mother at Bethune College. She was a BA
honors student in philosophy in 1936.

Because of Ma,

I have blossomed to be special.
I am Dr. Ferial Imam Haque. In my twenties I was honored with a
Doctor of philosophy degree in science
From the University of Strathclyde, Glasgow,
Scotland, United Kingdom, in 1970.

Ma's perseverance in her nineties set a shining example.
I am continuing my tough journey on the rough road
To be functional and productive in my golden age,
Striving for peace and to live in harmony in my community.

Same Family

We are three sisters who
Grew up under the loving care
Of our beloved mother.
She was unique in her ways
When parenting came into play!

Who can blame her?
She was a widow at twenty-five.
Well educated for her time
With a degree in philosophy,
She set her own rules
For her three daughters.
They would never cherish their father's love.

Her ideas were practical and unique.
Her slogan for women, young or old, was
To be independent, kind, and bold.
Persevere to attain your own identity to hold.

Her other slogan for women:
"It is better to have loved and lost
Than never to have loved at all."
Her three daughters traveled
With her wherever she went.

In 1950, she was a pioneer to venture on
A journey by plane and ship,
Crossing seas and oceans,
To reach her destination to London, England.
She was a scholar so brave and bold,
Her daughters tagging along.

Returning home in 1952 with honor and glory,
She had earned her master's degree in philosophy and
Joined as a professor in the department of philosophy
At Eden Girls' College in Dhaka City.

Education is the key element for a woman
To bloom and grow in order to give to society and thrive.
Her sincere and hard work
With many honors and much praise
From her homeland and abroad
Was an inspiration.

Mother and her three daughters after their
marriages in 1962 at her official residence,
Ruquayyah Hall, Dhaka University, where she served as Provost

Her three daughters are all well-educated and married.
They are professionals but did not neglect the family.
The eldest is a physician, the second is a chemist,
and the youngest is a physicist.
Mother is no longer with us, but the dash between
Two dates in her life, those of her birth and death,
Is indeed noteworthy!

This dash is remarkable, unprecedented, and unique.
It remains immortal to her family, as it will
For many generations to come.

May 26, 2014

My Two Sisters

It has been a long time since we left Ma's home.
The address: 6 Nilkhet Road, Dhaka, East Pakistan.
Ma's official residence as the provost of Women's Hall
University of Dhaka, East Pakistan.

It was in September 1963.
I was the last of Ma's three daughters to leave our home.
It had already been decided that after I left for Ottawa, Canada
As the wife of a Commonwealth Scholar to join my husband.
He was a graduate student at the University of Ottawa.
Ma would then leave for Nottingham University in England
To pursue her PhD program in Philosophy

My memories of school, college, and university days in this residence
Are varied, with happy times as well as trying
times for Ma and her three daughters.
We moved into this residence in 1957 when Ma joined the university
As founding provost of the first Women's Hall.

I have memories of growing up on the university campus
With Ma's ideology of education for women in the sixties.
Indeed, education does provide self-identity,
Independence, and economic freedom.
But she was also an advocate for marriage and family.
Her idea that husband and wife should be in the same profession
Is questionable and needs further research.

Anyway, she is credited for bringing up her
three daughters singlehandedly.
Being a widow in her twenties in the forties, fifties, and sixties,
She obtained her MA degree in philosophy as a part-time student

FERIAL IMAM HAQUE

From the University of Dhaka, British India.
To be independent financially, she was teaching at Eden Girls' School
With part-time and full-time help for
maintaining her three infant daughters.

কিম কন্যা- ৫ থেকে শিউলনর, ফেরিহান ও শারবাহার, ১৯৪৯

Three sisters in 1949
Left to right: older sister, the author, younger sister

She successfully completed her MA degree in 1947
And was awarded a prestigious scholarship to study abroad.
She pioneered her graduate studies in
London, England, in 1950–1952.
She demonstrated her responsibility as a loving mother:
Her three daughters accompanied her to England
While she pursued her studies. She earned her MA
Degree in philosophy from the London University in 1952.

We were fortunate to see, study, and speak the English language
At school In London, England, and we
spoke English amongst ourselves.

I developed a real fascination for learning
different languages at school:
Bengali, English, Urdu, and Arabic.
We spoke Bengali, English, Hindi, and Urdu with
Our peers, household helpers, and relatives.
I enjoyed art, music, sewing, knitting, cooking, and ironing.
At school I won three prizes each year for securing the
Second position in my class and first prizes
for both drawing and sewing.

I wanted to be an artist or an architect,
It was not possible for women to study in these fields,
My dreams could not be fulfilled.
So, I followed in the footsteps of our father.

Mother's wishes were that
One daughter would be a physician,
So, my older sister enrolled in the Medical College.
My younger sister and I followed in our father's footsteps.
My younger sister enrolled in physics, and I chose chemistry.
We successfully graduated with a B.Sc. Honors degree.

I was thrilled to draw diagrams or pictures whenever possible.
I loved drawing some of the pictures for my sister's biology lab book.
I recall my older sister studying most of the time.
Mother's friends at work offered to answer some of our questions
So we could get high grades on the exams.
Ma's wishes were that we would be the best in all avenues of learning.
My sister did her best to fulfill Ma's wishes
and earned her MBBS degree.
Soon after graduation in 1962 she married
her class friend, a medical doctor.
In winter 1963 she traveled to Oxford, England, to start her new job.
In the summer of 1963 her husband followed to join her.

I and my younger sister completed our final examinations
For BSc Honors degrees in science at the end of summer 1963,
Then we departed from Dhaka to join our husbands.
My sister's husband was in London, England.
She would pursue her graduate studies in physics.
And I traveled to Ottawa, Canada, to
My husband, who was a graduate student
In the Department of Chemistry,
University of Ottawa, Canada.

He was a Commonwealth Scholar,
So I came as the wife of a scholar and enjoyed some privileges.
Two-thirds of my return transportation was paid
By the Canadian government, and I was
given a monthly living allowance.
This ends the story of three sisters.

My childhood memories can be summed up in the following words:

The love in
Our family flows
Strong and deep,
Leaving us
Memories to
Treasure and keep.

—Author unknown

Prelude to Chapter 2

This chapter includes the narration of her memories of growing up in a faraway land in Ottawa, Canada, where she lived since 1963. The picture hanging on her bedroom wall tells the tale of her dreams as a teen in Dhaka, East Pakistan. Her Mother's inspiration and her conviction that a woman should live with dignity and an identity of her own in the global community was achievable through education. Being a migrant and dressing in her native costume, she managed to achieve her professional goals and complete all the chores of day-to-day living in many cities in different countries.

Chapter 2

Self

Be who you are and say what you feel, because those who mind don't matter, and those who matter don't mind.

—Bernard M. Birch

The Picture

The picture is half a century old.
It hangs on her bedroom wall.
The photographer captured the innocent teen's image
In black and white,
Not knowing who she would be
As part of the global community

The author in her teens as a first-year honors student
in chemistry, Dhaka University, 1960

After half a century!
She had two choices:
Education for self-identity or
Marriage to keep with the tradition of family.
She traveled the two roads to achieve her goals.

FERIAL IMAM HAQUE

She has sharp features, charming eyes, long black braided hair.
Earrings glitter, a gold necklace trims her neck, the
Tinkling sound of bracelets on her left arm,
A watch on her right wrist to keep time.
She was attractive, gracefully dressed in a sari, so beautiful.

She was an intelligent and studious student like her parents:
Mother was a philosopher, and Father was a physicist.
She studied chemistry, and the chemistry lab became her kitchen.
Her contributions are in pure and applied chemistry and
Forensic science. She is known internationally.

She returned to her birthplace in September 1970,
Having earned her PhD degree in chemistry
From Strathclyde University, Glasgow, Scotland.
She experienced the turbulence and turmoil of the liberation
Of Bangladesh on December 16, 1971.
Having survived the ordeal,
She, with her husband and child, returned to Ottawa
In July 1972 to be with the faces they'd known since 1963.

Her knowledge in science and her experiences
Of growing up in a family enriched with culture
Became the treasures she leveraged to earn a living.
She joined many groups so she could learn and become known
In her world of science and culture.
Multicultural groups in Ottawa
Drew her close and became her family.
They enriched Ottawa with a taste of
Diversity of culture in the seventies and eighties.

Indeed, the face of Ottawa has changed.
Language, dress, music, dance, art, culture, food.
Somerset Street West and Preston Street.
Houses, many ethnic shops, and restaurants.
We all know Chinatown and Little Italy.

Ottawa attracts tourists from everywhere during
Winterlude, the Tulip Festival, and Canada's birthday celebration.

Multicultural women's groups worked hard,
Dedicated many hours, to create halfway houses
For women and children
To escape from violence in the family.
Two of these are Harmony House and the
Nelson House of Ottawa-Carleton
In Ottawa, Ontario, Canada.

It was part of her dream of redefining the concept of a family home
Where the children would blossom and grow
With love, respect, and self-confidence
To be responsible citizens and
Proud Canadians in the global community.

My Dress

I'm a proud Canadian.
My dress attracts
Curious eyes wherever I go in Ottawa, and
Elsewhere I face many questions.

Question: Are you from India?
Reply: No.

Question: Oh! From Sri Lanka?
Reply: No.

Question: Then where are you from?
Reply: East Pakistan, which is Bangladesh now.

Question: When did you come here?
Reply: In 1963.

Question: How long have you been in Canada?
Reply: Since 1963.

Question: Do you always dress like this?
Reply: Yes.

Ferial in 1963 on her way to Ottawa, Canada

Question: Even in the winter?
Reply: Yes.

Question: Do you understand English?
Reply: Yes.

Question: Are you married?
Reply: Yes.

Question: Where does your husband work?
Reply: He is a student.

Reaction: Oh! Where?
Reply: Ottawa University.

Question: Do you work?
Reply: Yes.

FERIAL IMAM HAQUE

Reaction: [*with surprise*] Oh!
Reply: Yes. Why?

Question: Where do you work?
Reply: Carleton University.

Question: What do you do?
Reply: Research in chemistry.

The person becomes bewildered.

Question: Oh! Do they allow you to work like this?
Reply: Yes!

The conversation ends.
The bus stops at the bus stop.
I get up and get off the bus.

Dress

My birthplace is
East Bengal, British India.
On August 14, 1947, it became
Independent from the British rule.
Two independent nations were formed:
India and Pakistan.
The vast land of India separated Pakistan
Into West and East Pakistan.

Then came the change in Pakistan
Language, dress, food, and culture.
People in East Pakistan continued
To speak, read, and write in Bengali and
Dress in the sari, *salwar, kamiz,* and *orna.*

My childhood dress was a *frok* (dress),
Then I wore salwar, kamiz, and orna.
In my teen sari was my main form of dress
In school and at home in Dhaka.

When we were in London, England,
During the period 1950 to 1952,
I dressed in Western clothes.
Our school uniform at
Strand-on-the-Green School consisted of
Navy blue jeans, a white blouse,
Knee-high socks held with elastics,
Black shoes, and a hat called a beret.

When we returned to Dhaka, Bangladesh,
We dressed in the salwar, kamiz, and orna.

FERIAL IMAM HAQUE

In my teens the sari was my main dress.
At high school and university
In the science laboratories—
Physics, chemistry, botany, and zoology
All students wore a white lab coat
On top of their usual dress.

We faced no problems wearing the sari and
Traveling by school bus, rickshaw, or
Hackney carriage (a horse-drawn carriage).
We traveled by boats and ships—
Really, this was our usual costume.

My memories of learning to swim in a sari
In the pond at Women's Hall are unforgettable.
There was no life support belt/float.
Banana plants were used instead.

Sad to say, learning to swim
Was a total disaster and gave me many scary memories,
But I admired others in the group
Who learned to float and swim
With the banana plants to support them.

Adventure in a Crucible

(Memories of Half a Century)

June 21 is first day of summer.
We all like feeling the warmth of the sunshine.
No coats, no hat, no boots, no gloves,
No mittens, and no scarfs to wear.

The grass is green. So are the trees.
Flowers are blooming.
Birds are twittering,
Perched on trees.

The sky is clear, and all we hear are the
Songs of birds, the noise of cars.
People are walking and talking
While children are playing.

This day is so important in my life.
Why?
On this day I was born.
Wait, I say.
There is another important reason.

On this day I was awarded the honor of
Changing my name
From Ferial Haque to
Dr. Ferial Imam Haque.

Ferial Imam in 1970 in her PhD convocation gown in
Glasgow, Scotland, at Strathclyde University

I wondered why.
It was because of my sincere hard work, my research findings
In a small chemistry research laboratory
On the fourth floor of Thomas Graham Building.

Where is that? you may wonder.
In the Department of Pure and Applied Chemistry
On Cathedral Street, University of Strathclyde,
Glasgow, Scotland.

Here, I wrote a scientific book about molecules.
Day and night I read, thought, dreamed, and wrote.
I planned my experiment and gathered my equipment: glassware and
Chemicals—liquid and solid compounds in many forms.

At first I didn't know certain products were toxic,
So I became allergic and
Broke out in rashes and had respiratory problems,
Ending the story of my research

On my desk landed a new project.
With renewed hope and light,
I embarked on the new research
To find a solution to the unsolved mystery.

The challenge of this synthetic scheme was
To discover mystery of why
A certain lemon-yellow compound could not exist
At room temperature and room pressure.

Physical properties of this compound
Perplexed not only my mind but also the minds of other researchers,
Yet I was determined to continue
My earnest research to bring it into existence.

With persistence, I discovered
A very sensitive lemon-yellow compound
Extremely sensitive at room temperature and to air
With a shelf life of only a few seconds.

So, I was delighted to get this clue.
My thoughts and imagination gave me some
Hope to create a special chamber
Where its lifetime could be extended.

Now my task was to establish its identity.
It was called π-cycloheptadienylmanganese tricarbonyl.
When I found the right chamber,
I thought it was like an incubator.

In an incubator a premature life grows and thrives.
I succeeded in my quest to prove the existence of

FERIAL IMAM HAQUE

π-cycloheptadienylmanganese tricarbonyl, something
My predecessors could not achieve.

I got the green light to complete my book.
Many experiments I designed and carried out
To conclude the story of the existence of
The mysterious lemon-yellow compound.

I held the round-bottomed flask with this compound
Under inert conditions in a vacuum. I gazed.
It is you! I had the power to grasp and accomplish
My goal to change my status in society
To become a member of the Scientific Society.

My book stands on the bookshelves
In the library of Strathclyde University and around the world.
It also claims its position on bookshelves
Of researchers in the field around the world.

This book's title is
The Influence of Iron and Manganese Carbonyl
On the Reactivity of Cyclic Seven-Membered Organic Ligands.
The compound is unique and very sensitive,
but it attracts many researchers.

I am a daydreamer seeking to solve unsolved problems
In the chemistry research laboratories of
The global scientific community.
The lab is where I lived as a student and researcher and employee.

So, with this knowledge I embarked on many projects
Encompassing environmental and synthetic chemistry.
Last but not the least, I became anchored to
Find ways to reveal latent fingerprints
At crime scenes to solve murder mysteries.

The Glowing Lemon-Yellow Color

In my clothes closet, the yellow sweater brought back
Memories of my research laboratory in the
Department of Pure and Applied Chemistry
At the University of Strathclyde, Glasgow, Scotland.

I was a female PhD student in 1968.
Students are faced with the challenge to discover
Or prove the identity of a new compound.
My project was on synthetic organometallic chemistry
To prove the existence of a compound called
π-cycloheptadienylmanganese tricarbonyl.

This lemon-yellow compound brought about a change in
My status so I could join the world of science.
I accepted the challenge to prove its existence.
With my dedication to learning and working long hours
In the research laboratory, I proved its existence.

Scientists would like to know how I succeeded.
After many long hours of work in the laboratory,
I obtained a viscous lemon-yellow product.
It was in a round-bottomed flask capped with a special stopper.
I gazed at the product, making notes in the lab book.

I stored the flask in the refrigerator and visited the library, where I
Sat quietly in a corner to review the notes and publications.
Suddenly, it dawned on my mind that maybe it was hygroscopic.
Why don't I observe its properties under low vacuum?
My task now was to crystallize it into its solid form in inert condition.

I went to the laboratory and took the flask from the refrigerator.
Gazing at the bright lemon-yellow non-crystalline compound,

I recited a few words to become inspired
and then embarked on my plan.
I connected the flask to a vacuum, gazing at the product.
Then slowly I opened the stopcock to
increase the water pump pressure.

I let the flask sit for a while, thinking of alternative
ways to solidify the compound.
An hour later I could not see a major change,
So I turned off the vacuum, still anxiously gazing at the product.
Slowly turning on the vacuum, I observed after a while
Some movement in the viscous compound.
I could see some solid compound in the flask!

I got up from my stool and walked around in my space.
Keeping my fingers crossed, I came back and picked up the flask.
I was astounded and whispered, "I have got it! I have got it!"
The next day I announced this to my professor. He came to inspect.
He took the flask and gazed at it with surprise. In a low voice
He said, "Please take it to the Analytical Lab downstairs.
Tell the supervisor to do the analysis in-house immediately."

Immediately, I went and asked to see the supervisor and
Relayed my professor's instructions for elemental analysis.
I filled out the required form to complete the official formalities.
Then I returned to my desk and recorded all pertinent information
In my lab book, not knowing what the future outcome would be.

The next day I got the results and showed them to my professor.
With a sigh of relief he said,
Now you can repeat all the experiments you did before.
I knew once I had completed those steps,
I could begin to wrap up the project and embark on the story.

It is my adventurous journey with the flasks, playing with
Many solids and liquids, like cooking in my kitchen and preparing
My meals for lunch and supper with lots of imagination.

The thesis is the story of my dream and honest and hard work,
Introducing my new concepts to adding to the previous findings.

This is an account of my dream and my goal to pioneer as a woman
To demonstrate that gender is not a restriction to achieving
Any dream and revealing the secrets of the unknown.
The only difference is in how to establish a common way to
Discuss problems and successes on our journey together
With my supervisor to reach our final goal.

The story of my findings I recorded in a thesis
As a requirement for the degree. Then
I was honored with the doctorate of philosophy.
When my name was called, I climbed the stairs to the stage,
Dressed in the special bluish-colored gown.
I was trembling, perhaps with excitement, and received the diploma.

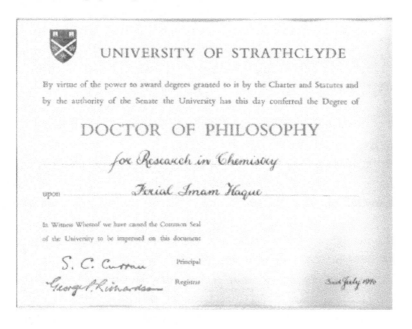

Ferial Imam's PhD diploma awarded by the University
of Strathclyde, Glasgow, Scotland, 1970

After that my journey was like a roller-coaster ride.
Finally, I came to the decision to settle in Ottawa.
Here I am today, recapping the days and relating my memories of
Growing up and taking active part to change the face of Ottawa
Canada's capital, where I enjoy the many
cultures and flavors brought by
The diversity of people.

Elements Are Dancing in the Flask—A Chemical Reaction

Memories take me back to the year 1968. It was summer in Glasgow, Scotland. I was in the Department of Pure and Applied Chemistry Research Laboratory, Strathclyde University.

The weather in Glasgow was so unpredictable. I had to get used to sunshine and the sudden ghastly wind blowing my umbrella away from me. I got wet, but I continued to walk toward the chemistry laboratory assigned to me.

As I entered the main entrance to the building, the security guard greeted me. It became a routine to pick up my bottle of milk and proceed to the elevator. As soon as the elevator door opened, I stepped in and pressed the button for the fourth floor. Professor Stevenson was in the elevator. He took off his hat and greeted me.

The elevator door opened on the fourth floor. I stepped out, heading toward my locker to store my coat and broken umbrella. Of course, I put on my lab coat and my shoes and proceeded to my space in the laboratory.

The cleaning woman greeted me and asked curiously, "How did you manage in the ghastly wind this morning?"

I replied with much disappointment, "Oh! My umbrella almost blew away from my hand. It turned inside out."

I was comforted with her kind words and wisdom. She said, "What I do is just turn the opposite away from the blowing wind. The wind blows the umbrella back to its original form."

I delightfully expressed my gratitude for this bit of practical wisdom by exclaiming, "Oh! Thank you so much."

She continued with her responsibilities of wiping all the bottles and jars containing the chemicals. I began to follow my routine for the day.

I got busy setting up the experiment in the fume hood for the synthesis of the dimanganesedecacarbonyl, which is a lengthy experiment. I ensured the chemicals required—methylcymentrene, metallic sodium, carbon monoxide, and diglyme/dioxane—were all

FERIAL IMAM HAQUE

ready for the experiment the next day. I would need to start early to complete all the steps to obtain the desired compounds. So, I did not start anything new and left early for home and prepare for the early next day.

Becoming a Writer

Why do I wish to write?
As I was growing up, I heard
Many different sounds of words
In many languages and dialects
Spoken at home by people around.

Early in the morning I would hear the
Cock crowing, sitting on the huge wood-apple tree,
Grandfather reciting from
The Holy Qur'an in his melodious voice,
The housekeeper in her unique dialect
Calling us to get ready for school.

As the day progressed, other helpers
Arrived to perform their duties for the day,
Speaking in the language and dialect of their choice.
Some I would understand; with others, I was lost.
But Mother had to understand them all!

When it was time to enroll at school, I knew
The dialect of the Bengali would be the written version,
Comparable to the King's English and not Cockney!
Languages we studied were Bengali, English, Urdu, and Arabic.
What fun! English and Bengali we would write from left to right.
With Urdu and Arabic, we would begin from
the right and write toward the left.

It was great to be able to speak so many languages.
I must credit little old me for being a master of these
Languages, both written and spoken, at home and at school.
Translating the three languages into Bengali was fun.
At the end of the day I was so happy because everything was done.

FERIAL IMAM HAQUE

Writing became second nature at school.
It became more interesting as I learned the many
Symbols in chemistry as I memorized the periodic table.
How thrilled I was when I used different symbols
Of the elements to write different words in symbols.
Water is H_2O, salt is $NaCl$, oxygen is O_2, and nitrogen is N_2.

How interesting it became to observe, record, and infer
The findings of the experiments in physics and chemistry.
I was amazed to discover how quickly I mastered the skill to
Find words when writing the conclusion of each experiment,
Both in physics and chemistry, becoming so comfortable.

Later in my life as I participated in social issues,
I became interested in my skills with and knowledge of
Science to solve the problems of the day-to-day life chores
In the kitchen and in the areas of health,
transportation, and gardening.
I moved on to solving more complex problems in society,
Such as solving crime for the justice system.
I am reading the introductory paragraph of
The murder mystery story "Dr. Inertia."

Ferial reading during her book launch in Hamilton in January 1998

I would always look for groups to nurture my interests.
I communicate through words and share
with other writers in my group.
I, as a member of
The new writing workshop in 1997, had two
stories in an anthology published by
The Jasper Press and edited by Chris Pannell
entitled *Between a Dock and a High Place.*
That was my first experience
Reading before an audience during the book launch
In Hamilton in January 1998!

A Tale of Happiness

My story "A Tale of Happiness" describes the challenge to prove my knowledge to reach my long-standing goal to complete my doctoral degree in chemistry.'

I embarked on my journey to reach my dream. So, I titled the situation as follows:

Crystallization of Knowledge
Doctoral Studies

The story of my success as a scientist began after I left Ottawa for Glasgow with my husband at the end of January 1968. I was determined to acquire a better degree within a minimal amount of time. I always reminded myself of the motivational words of great people: "Every cloud has a silver lining" and "Failures are the pillars of success." I cannot forget the inspirational saying of Francis Bacon: "Knowledge is power." Since September 1963 I had been away from my country and family. I had been living in Ottawa, Ontario, Canada, with none of my family members or people from the Indo-Pakistani culture. My life revolved around love and searching for intellectual growth. I was young, bright, and knowledgeable, I thought, having completed my BSc honors exams in chemistry at the University of Dhaka, East Pakistan. I was proud of myself and thought how lucky I was to have memories of living in London, England, for two years with my mother in the early fifties. I had no difficulty communicating in English with the professors, staff, and other students at the university.

We embarked on the British Overseas Airways Corporation plane from Dorval, Montreal, heading to Prestwick, Scotland. We were greeted by my husband's new supervisor at the airport and were escorted to the center of the city of Glasgow. We settled down in an apartment and then began our journey toward a new life with many challenges. Soon I became acquainted with the surroundings where we were living. It was hard to adjust to the new city of Glasgow with its striking differences in architecture, roads, stores, and shopping areas. In contrast to Ottawa, the buildings were dull with very little space for gardens. The roads were narrow and windy and crowded with so many people. The stores were small like the country grocer's with signs: Greengrocer, Butcher, Fish Market, and many more.

I will never forget my interview with Professor P. L. Pauson, head of the Department of Organic and Organometallic Chemistry in the Department of Pure and Applied Chemistry, Strathclyde University, on Cathedral Street, Glasgow. Professor Pauson's small stature attracted my attention. He was slim and short.

On the day of the appointment, I knocked on his office door, and he greeted me, welcoming me into his office. I took a quick glance around his office and saw that the layout was comfortable. On the left-hand side near the window was his huge executive desk and chair. The desk was piled with neatly arranged files, papers, books, pencils and pens, plus a telephone. All around the walls were glass-fronted bookshelves with neatly arranged books, journals, and reference materials. Near the widow were vinyl-covered sofas, and at the center of the office were two huge tables with chairs around them.

Very soon I was invited to sit on the vinyl sofa, and then he sat down. He asked me about my background and interests. I explained my intentions of getting a PhD degree. He paused and moved to the blackboard and began to write a few chemical reactions. He made it clear that there was funding available for this research; he would be able to support me if I decided to undertake this project. My immediate reaction was to gladly accept to work on this project. But I did bring up my concern about the minimum time in which I wished to complete the thesis and all other requirements.

Without hesitation, Professor Pauson replied, "I cannot foresee any problems as twenty-one months is the minimum time required for the submission of a PhD thesis."

I accepted the offer, but with much surprise I said, "I will accept the offer, but my knowledge of organometallic chemistry is shallow."

Before I left his office, he handed me his book on organometallic chemistry and said, "Read this." I looked at the cover page and realized that he was the Father of Organometallic Chemistry.

Professor P. L. Pauson led me to one of his research laboratories where he occasionally worked. There was room for only six research students.

The space near the window facing west of the building became my place to study, do experiments, and record my findings in the laboratory notebook. Now I think back and say that it was my kitchen for doing the experiments to synthesize new compounds. This was where I completed my dream degree, a PhD in chemistry, in 1970.

Prelude to Chapter 3

This chapter shows how Ferial adjusted to the new way of life in Ottawa, Canada, in 1963, after having been greeted by the host family to create her new self and discover her new life. Many decades have passed since. Then in late 2015, she attempted to find the meaning of life. In the sixties way, she learned the differences in the Canadian education system and Canadian culture, and she adjusted to her husband's concept of life and family. Life was so different then without modern technology and telecommunication. Then came the experience of motherhood alone in Ottawa. She then juggled the role of a mother and wife, along with the responsibilities of a graduate student. Subsequently she discovered human nature.

Chapter 3

Life

Life is not about finding yourself. Life is about creating yourself.

—George Bernard Shaw

February 4, 2018

My New Year's Wish

My New Year's wish
Entails a long list so hard to finish!
I shudder to find there are no funds
To cover the costs for anything I wish.

I wonder why.
Is it because now I am old and
Can't go out to work in the cold?
Is this why my wish list is not complete?

I wonder why I can't have a wish list like my husband.
The only difference is that we are not of the same gender.
He is a man and has a pension.
Being a woman, I am without one.

I only get paid when I work.
That is what I accepted when I decided to earn a living.
So! I can't buy my winter coat, boots, or gloves, or a sweater.
I can't go out in the cold, windy, white winter days.

Fate has parted us, as he is in a nursing home.
He spends time in a special wheelchair and rests in bed.
The staff bathe and dress him and transfer him
With special equipment from bed to wheelchair.

He tells me he has no brain, but
The staff say he needs a three-piece suit.
"Oh!" I say. "What about his wife of fifty years?
Where will she stay? What will she eat and wear?"

FERIAL IMAM HAQUE

So, my investment of time, work, and earnings
Has all been in vain!
Where is my right to live in the city where I worked
For more than half a century to make it a better place?!

We live with people who have come from many corners of the world
With diverse backgrounds and different
tastes in food, dress, and language.
We enjoy walking in Little Italy and Chinatown
On Preston Street and Somerset Street West in Ottawa.

Sometimes, I come to a dead end and I
Can see the lights bright and red.
I pause to think and take a deep breath.
I get up and say, "I must search for my wealth."

I am looking for my precious health,
Hoping the days ahead in the coming years
Will bring back my health and wealth
So I can strive for *peace* and live in good health!

Sweetland Avenue

In the year 1963
I came to Ottawa as a wife,
A new bride, to join my husband.
My husband was Canadian Commonwealth
Scholar, a PhD student in the
Department of Chemistry at the
University of Ottawa.

Wow! I thought, once I learned that
Spouses were entitled to an allowance
From the Canadian government,
Two-thirds of their return passage fare,
And all medical expenses paid.

My travel arrangements were made
By the travel agent in Dhaka, East Pakistan.
The return ticket was given to me.
The travel itinerary was well planned.

It was a long journey from Dhaka via Karachi to London, England,
I flew from Dhaka Airport to Karachi Airport
In West Pakistan by the Pakistan International Airlines.
At Karachi Airport I changed aircraft operated by
British Overseas Airways Corporation
On my way to London, England.
A stopover either in the Middle East or Europe.

I made a stopover in London, England
To spend a few days with my two sisters
And their families,
One sister was living in London and
The other sister in Oxford, England.
I enjoyed my journey alone so far.

Real life began when I said goodbye
To my two sisters at the London airport.
I embarked on a BOAC airplane
My way to Dorval Airport in Quebec, Canada.

Ferial in Ottawa in 1964

My cheeks were wet. I wiped my tears
With my handkerchief so carefully ironed.
I sat in my seat alone. The one beside me was empty.
There were not too many passengers.

Looking out the window, gazing below, I saw
It was beautiful outside, but my heart was empty.
When the plane rose above the clouds,
I took my shoes off and
Made myself comfortable with my legs
Curled up on the seat.
I covered myself with the gorgeous red shawl
Embroidered with golden thread.

Slowly I dozed off.
My mind was filled with so many unknowns.
How would I survive alone
With my husband, whom I hardly knew.

Oh! How would I survive the long winter with its snow?
And so many more unknowns.
Each day of the year for about four years
I wondered how difficult it would be to
Walk on the deep-snow-covered pavement.
I did not know in Canada *pavement* meant sidewalk.

I was tired and fell asleep on the two seats.
A voice woke me up.
All I heard was "It is time to eat.
What would you like, chicken or beef?"
In surprise I must have said, "Chicken."
Again I dozed off.

The air hostess came and set up the folding table.
Soon came the carefully arranged food on a tray.
I am sure I enjoyed my food as it reminded me
Of my school dinners in the fifties in London.

Our plane, a Boeing 707, was
Flying above the clouds, traveling west
Over the Atlantic Ocean to the
East coast of Canada.

I was tired and alone in the plane, not knowing
What the weather would be like in Canada.
If memory serves me, it was sunny and cool
But not freezing cold, either in Dorval Airport or
At Ottawa Airport when the small plane landed
It was small, for only domestic flights.

FERIAL IMAM HAQUE

My host family and students greeting me at the small
domestic Ottawa airport, September 1963

My heart was beating fast as I did not know
Who would come with my husband
To receive me or what the plans were.
I was delighted to see the host family
With a few graduate students.

I was cordially greeted by everyone.
They drove us to the apartment,
W dropped off our luggage and I changed my clothes.
We visited the host family for supper.
I was so glad to have a home-cooked meal.

After supper they drove us to
Our small apartment,
58 Sweetland Avenue, Apt. No. 2.
I felt a vacuum in my heart
As it was the first time I'd ever stayed
With a male gender—my husband!

It was the beginning of a new journey,
A new life! It was full of surprises each day:
New way of life, new education system,
Independent banking, settling into university, and
Buying winter clothes, food, and stationery.
That was my rough beginning to become a new me.
This is the tale of my experiences every day.

Riding on Bus #4

My memories of riding on bus #4 in 1964 to Carleton University in the Glebe from Sandy Hill near the University of Ottawa campus are unforgettable.

Ferial in her camel hair coat in December 1963 at
Parliament Hill, Ottawa, Canada's capital

My address was 58 Sweetland Avenue, apartment no. 2. The bus stop was down the hill at the foot of Sweetland Avenue on Somerset Street East. The journey was one hour or longer, depending on the travel time of the day.

Early each weekday morning I dressed in my sari and winter clothing: woolen sweater, scarf, camel hair coat, fur hat, leather mittens, boots, and lots of handkerchiefs. I carried my handbag and two other bags. One bag was packed with chemistry textbooks, exercise books, a pencil case, a slide rule (calculators were not yet in existence), students' assignments, and my laboratory manual.

In another bag was my supply of food for the day: sandwich, cake/cookies, and fruits neatly packed in paper sandwich bags (no water bottles fifty years ago, so one less heavy thing to carry).

I was a graduate student in the Chemistry Department. All graduate students were employed as research and teaching assistants and thus were provided with a source of income to cover tuition, fees, and living expenses. My duties, like those of the other assistants, were to correct assignments and demonstrate techniques for the laboratory curriculum.

Walking to the bus stop from Sweetland Avenue was scary but adventurous. I took small steps to walk down Sweetland Avenue. It was steep and covered with soft and fluffy white snow. Walking on the snow was fun fifty years ago. The scenes from the movie *Little Women* came alive and became vivid as I plowed through the snow dressed in my sari. I stepped forward, but it felt like I slipped back a few inches with each step, so I decided to leave earlier to make up the lost time.

With my heavy luggage I would stop, put my two bags on the snow to rest, and look around to cherish the relaxing serenity of the white snow. I could not take my eyes off this scene, but soon I realized I must hurry; otherwise I would miss bus #4. The wait in the cold would be another twenty minutes for the next #4 bus.

The thought of missing the bus did not bother me as I enjoyed the outdoor scene and fresh air, the trees covered with snow swaying in the gentle breeze, the branches swinging in a rhythmic way.

Standing at the bus stop I could see the headlights of bus #4 glowing and getting brighter as it approached the bus stop. I picked up my bags and dusted off the snow, ready to get on bus #4 when it stopped. The door opened, and the driver waited for me to climb the two steps. I put the bags on the first step, got up, put the bags on the next step, then stepped inside the bus with my bags.

I found a seat at the front near the entrance. It was an automatic choice because in my country women sit near the driver for safety and protection. I put my bus ticket in the box, picked up the bags, and sat down.

Bus #4 slowly moved to its next stop, at the corner of King Edward Avenue and Somerset Street East. Then came the stop in front of the Vanier Science Library; across the street was the Chemistry Department.

Bus #4 turned right on Nicholas Street. It stopped at the intersection of Laurier Avenue East behind Tabaret Hall, the administration faculty building of the University of Ottawa.

Nicholas Street ended at Rideau Street at the traffic light in front of the entrance of Caplan's Department Store. The family of a graduate student in the Department of Chemistry owned this department store.

My first shopping stop was at Caplan's Department Store when I first arrived in Ottawa in September 1963, to buy my camel hair winter coat, winter boots, and gloves—all the winter clothing—to face the unknown hazards of an Ottawa snowstorm.

Sitting next to the window on bus #4, I saw at the corner of Nicholas and Rideau Streets the entrance to the main building of the Charles Ogilvy department store. The furniture and home décor of this store was located at the corner of Besserer Street and Nicholas Street.

Bus #4 turned left on Rideau Street in front of Caplan's Department Store. We drove past Freeman's Department Store, now the home of the Hudson Bay Department Store.

The intersection of Sussex Drive and Rideau Street reflects my memories of my first bank account and safety deposit box for safekeeping of my wedding jewelry, at the bank on the left side of Rideau Street. The Elephant and Castle restaurant now stands there.

Diagonally across at the corner of Sussex Drive stood the Chateau Laurier Hotel; on the opposite side was Union Station. Now it is the conference center. The Chateau Laurier and Union Station were connected by an underground tunnel.

Sweet are the memories of being the guest of the Honorable Speaker of Pakistan at the Chateau Laurier Hotel in 1965 for lunch. The Speaker, who was from my hometown, Dhaka, was in Ottawa to attend the Commonwealth Conference.

He missed Bengali meals, and there were no Indian, Pakistani, or Bengali restaurants in Ottawa at that time. I was contacted by the second secretary of the Pakistan High Commission (a graduate of Dhaka University like me and my husband) to see if I had time to prepare a typical Bengali lunch at his official apartment.

(I remember my husband came home with requests from different Bengali men from undivided India because they missed typical Bengali meals and there was a limited number of Bengali families in Ottawa. One gentleman from his village wished to have spinach and shrimp; another person, daal curry with tomatoes and chili; another, fish curry and boiled rice. We were all homesick as there were very few people from East and West Bengal.)

Cooking had been my hobby since childhood, and being a synthetic organic chemist, I enjoyed cooking with the ingredients that were available. The supply of ingredients and the selection of fresh fish was limited. We would buy our meat from Albert Meat Market in the Byword Market.

After listening to what the Honorable Speaker wished to have, I suggested the menu below so I would be able to cook within the specified time. Remember, in those days there was no microwave oven in the kitchen.

Palau, plain rice
Herring fish curry
Shrimp and spinach
Beef with cabbage curry
Potato bharta
Daal curry with tomatoes and chilies
Special hot tomato salad

As bus #4 drove on Wellington Street, we could see on Elgin Street the elegant Lord Elgin Hotel, which still attracts tourists from around the world. On Wellington Street we passed Parliament Hill on the right. The United States Embassy was across the street.

Bus #4 turned left on Bank Street, going southbound. The ride was long as the bus stopped at every stop to drop off and pick up passengers traveling to and from the Glebe and surrounding residential areas. Bank Street was one of the main shopping areas then with stores like Beamish and Eaton and many specialty stores, including India Import at the corner of Gilmour Street. Near Somerset Street West was the Rialto movie theater (entrance tickets there were the cheapest in town).

We continued on Bank Street and turned right on Catherine Street, stopping at the Voyageur/Greyhound bus terminal. We traveled on Catherine Street and turned left on Bronson Avenue. We passed Carling Avenue on the right and Glebe Collegiate Institute on the left.

Soon we came to the bridge over Dow's Lake, where the world-renowned Tulip Festival takes place. Who knew that I would be a member of the organizing committee for the city festivities as vice president of the Ottawa Folk Arts Council in 1976?!

We drove past Sunnyside Avenue on the left. On the right was snow in winter and green meadow in summer. The main entrance to Carleton University was located opposite Brewer Park, where the field house and Alumni Hall are situated now. The last stop for bus #4 and bus #7 was near the entrance of University Centre, the cafeteria, and the tunnel connecting all the buildings.

In 1964 the science faculty was housed in the Tory Building. The Chemistry Department was on the fourth floor; biology, the fifth floor; and physics, the second floor. And on the First Avenue campus a few other departments of the science faculty operated. Social sciences was in Paterson Hall. Southam Hall housed all lecture rooms and lecture theaters, and there was MacOdrum Library. There were a few residences, some for male students and others for female students.

The quad was neatly landscaped with a green lawn and birch trees, and the squirrels were great company at lunchtime while I enjoyed my lunch under the birch trees. Convocations were held at the quad. In summertime I enjoyed the natural beauty of the Carleton campus. On sunny days I would walk to other side of the Rideau River with a group of students from the lab to have lunch. These are the memories bonding me to Carleton University and its campus.

Other universities I attended are Dhaka University, East Pakistan; Strathclyde University, Glasgow, Scotland; University of Ottawa, Canada; and Georgia State University, Atlanta, Georgia, USA.

This is taken from *Our Lives*, volume 2, about the history of the group and how it came into being.

The Riviera Writers joined together in the winter of 2009–2010 after taking a memoir writing course at Carleton University, Ottawa, where they had met. In the spring of 2010 they issued a compilation of their memoirs entitled *Our Lives*. In June 2014 they prepared this second compilation. This is *not for public distribution*.

FERIAL IMAM HAQUE

As I Remind Myself

I was born a daughter
To accept the social rituals,
But nobody has the final say on
How my heart wants to play.
Yet I can't forget I have grown
To become a professional woman
Living in a faraway land in another country.

My parents, looking at me from up above,
Will be content although I am not a son.
Yet I have tried my best to give.
However little scope I was given,
I have tried to find ways to reveal the latent fingerprints
For the justice department as a forensic scientist.

I will pay my tribute to my parents in
Whatever way I am able to do as a woman.
I will remember you both on
Special days, sad or happy!
I am proud to be who I am today.

Thank you both for enlightening my heart
With your wisdom as professionals.
Father, you are a physicist,
And Mother, you are a philosopher.
I am only survivor from the battlefield.
I am proud to be a forensic scientist.
I strive for peace and harmony as a migrant.

A New Lifestyle

Memories are like
The amazing phase diagram
Of nature's essential gift of water.
It changes its form with temperature

To solid, liquid, and gas.
We also change with time,
And within our given boundaries we
Make the best use of our time and
Intelligence to create our self-identity
To be in touch with our family, our
Friends, and the global community.

After fifty-five years, it seems to me that
Health restrictions call for a change.
A new lifestyle becomes mandatory if we wish
To move on in life and maintain our productivity,
Being happy and content as long as we can.

April 11, 2017

Different Views of Three Minds

I have come to realize that as sisters,
We are different, yet we grew up
Under our mother's discipline and care.
We believed and accepted many social ways and were taught
To welcome family traditions without any question.

We three sisters realized education is an essential
Component of a girl's life if she is to face the changing world ahead
In the twentieth and twenty-first century. So true then and today!
We accepted mother's family tradition and
embraced it to welcome marriage,
So nobody could declare Mother's daughters were old maids!

Time told the story of each of her three daughters' lives.
They were each in different countries,
separated by the Atlantic Ocean,
Busy creating their own lives to be the people they wanted to be.
In a new land they were destined to create a new self.

My tale of life began in the year 1963 after my wedding.
A year before, I was naive about the complexity of global society.
Yet, like an adventurer, in my early twenties I embraced the adventure.
I embarked on the long journey from Dhaka,
East Pakistan, with a stopover
To be with my sisters in London and Oxford, England.
I remember feeling special and brave for facing the Canadian winter
And to accept my husband, whom I hardly knew as a person.

When I stepped out of a small plane at the
Ottawa Airport, which was so small,

And as I climbed down the steps, my heart
was beating fast, it seemed.
I was going to meet a group of unfamiliar people in a different setting.
I could not foresee the unknown destination
of my journey as a young bride.
Without fear I walked toward the crowd
with only one familiar face, that of
My husband! Others were graduate students and the host family.
I was greeted by everyone in the group. My
subconscious mind was whispering,
Be brave and gracious. Accept all invitations to
things they have planned, and enjoy!

It was a sunny day in early September 1963 with a gentle cool breeze.
I could not comfort myself with thoughts of how
I would settle down with my husband
In a new land with new plans to build my new self and
To create my new identity in order to keep
moving to reach my goal and dream.

I looked beyond my childhood days and stretched my limits
To gain new experiences, defining my new self,
So I would never need to return to my old dimensions.
I had to find new ways to bloom and thrive in this new land.

Sisters, we were separated for a reason unknown.
That I will never know, although I could
find ways to pave a new path and
Travel on it to meet and embrace my sisters
to reveal our new identities.
I had confidence and respect for my inner self,
as I could answer many concerns
About science and society.

I embarked on a project to stop drug trafficking in 1979 in Ottawa.
Today in Canada marijuana is legal for certain
people with health conditions,
Within strict legal boundaries. But like other drugs users,
These people will not be spared from the harmful side effects.

About four decades ago I dedicated my research skills
To finding ways to develop new methods to reveal
The latent fingerprints of perpetrators in order to stop crime.
With this confidence, I wondered why I could not embark
On another predominant project, that of stopping family quarrels.
Domestic disputes lead to marriage breakdown,
creating insecurity for children
And their mothers, bringing them down from riches to poverty.

Sisters, I held you so dear and near to my heart
Over the many decades, *hoping* that some day
We would be together to rejoice in the results of each of our
New characters, knowledge, and professional dreams.
We would then anchor our ideology to the ideology of our parents.
I earnestly made many attempts when Mother said goodbye
To us all, finding her new place to rest in peace for eternity
without any remorse.
So, my sisters, I hope soon will we try to accept one another
With respect and love for who we are today,
Not create family quarrels to be settled in court.

Dear sisters, you believe in leaving behind the past deeds of people,
Good or bad, without any gratitude for the person
Who stood by you amid the dire legal battles to
Settle the lingering dispute our elders left
To us, their successors.

Sisters, you and your lawyers were remarkable
To end this twisted litigation that
Hung in the air for many decades.
Mother and her siblings could not benefit from

The wealth that was left by their parents.
The family quarrel intensified and continued to linger on.

Are we three sisters going to squabble on?
Are we going to fight about who I am and
why I must change my personality?
I can't forget my experiences of creating my new self and identity,
Having survived the war and fleeing the war zone
In my birth country and workplace in Dhaka in 1972.
It was the early seventies at the Dhaka University campus!

We grew up to be who we are today to show our parents' families
What a remarkable job our beloved mother did in bringing us up
Under her umbrella of care to protect her three daughters
From unforeseen disasters that could drown us in tears.
As a chemist, I can see the result of our hard work every day.
Today, each one of us has bloomed into a
beautiful and unique personality.

I can never learn to adapt the ways of yesterday
To crush the tender feelings of my new self
I formed while dreaming of a new life in a new country,
In the process having mastered many skills
to survive many challenges,
Having survived the war and left behind all belongings
To begin a new life in a new country as an immigrant.

We three sisters should be proud of our individual identities,
Bearing in mind that we can't mimic Mother's ways.
Our struggles in our lives in a foreign land are so different,
Requiring us to acquire knowledge of the laws of the land and of
The culture, language, climate, and communication—and more.

I had to make many unconventional decisions,
Being a woman when the world was not prepared
To provide women equal status as men.
But gradually women have campaigned and made

An impact on the global stage to demonstrate
Women are people. We have voting rights
To solve political, health, scientific, and social problems.

The history of International Women's Day
Demonstrates the progress women have achieved,
Moving forward each day in every profession to
Obtain our goal, to reach equal pay for our time.
Let us learn from this enlightening example
To jump out of the orbit of traditional thinking.
Let us live in harmony in the family, within
society, and internationally!
Let us rejoice in the dedicated efforts of women over the centuries.

Prelude to Chapter 4

In this chapter, the author narrates how she was inspired in her childhood through music. In London, England, she was exposed to inspirational songs in her choir group and became fascinated with inspirational songs in Bengali, Urdu, and Hindi. The lyrics of great minds—their chosen words—made a great impact on her mind and inspired her to maintain her momentum as a person.

Chapter 4

Inspirational Memories

Hope is being able to see that there are light despite all the darkness.

—Desmond Tutu

February 4, 2018 (edited)

My New Year's Dream

Being away from my birthplace and
Coming to Ottawa, Canada, in 1963,
I was the wife of a Commonwealth Scholar
With many hopes and dreams.

Wow! Time flies.
I recall my childhood song
At school, Strand-on-the-Green,
In London, England, in 1950:

"Time, you old gypsy man,
Will you not stay?
Put up your caravan
Just for one day?"

Way back in 1963, I did not come to stay.
I set up a home for a few years
While we were graduate students
At the universities in Ottawa, Canada.

My dreams. "How wonderful it will be!"
In the new city of Ottawa, in a new country
With my husband, whom I hardly knew, I had
Sweet thoughts: *He will love and care for me!*

With the flow of time like a tidal wave,
My dreams were washed away in my tears.
Yet I stood alone and free. With my eyes closed,
I took a deep breath and said,

"I am here today! Where will I be tomorrow?"

FERIAL IMAM HAQUE

Oh yes! I, like the gypsy man,
Traveled to many countries and
Lived in many cities:
London, England; Glasgow, Scotland;
Atlanta, Georgia, USA; Ottawa, Canada.

Of course, I cannot be in my birthplace
In Chittagong, British India.
I, along with my two sisters, grew up in Dhaka,
Capital of East Bengal, British India, which was divided
Into two countries, India and Pakistan, in 1947.

On August 14, 1947, Pakistan became independent.
The word *Pakistan* means "holy country."
The vast land of India separated Pakistan into
West Pakistan and East Pakistan.

The capital of West Pakistan was Peshawar, and
That of East Pakistan was Dhaka.
The two parts were culturally different.
The state language was Urdu, and the state religion was Islam.

I was fortunate to learn four languages at school—
Bengali, Urdu, English, and Arabic—in East Pakistan,
Although our mother tongue was Bengali.
East Pakistan was liberated on December 16, 1971,
Occupying the space on the world map now known as Bangladesh.

On New Year's Day 2013
I ask myself many questions:
Where is my home? Am I like the gypsy man?
Where are my parents? Where are my sisters?
Where are our daughters? And where is my husband?
First and foremost, who am I? And what have I done?

So many answers to too many questions,
All cluttered in my mind.

I realize that I am a proud Canadian
Living in Ottawa. Now it is my home.

My dear father bid farewell to the world
When I was a toddler, on December 24, 1943.
Father's final resting place is in his hometown of Comilla.
I was not allowed to visit his grave because I was a little girl.

Our responsible mother said goodbye in 2009.
It was on June 22. Now she is resting peacefully
In Mirpur graveyard in Dhaka.
On the head post is written the two dates:
Her date of birth, December 30, 1917, and,
After a Dash, June 22, 2009, the day she took her final breath.

Mother led an active life until her ninetieth birthday,
Leaving behind so many legacies
Housed in her estate museum and foundation.
Many discussions, lectures, and annual meetings are
Held in the auditorium next to the museum.
My two sisters have been living in London, England
On the East coast of Canada separated
By the vast Atlantic Ocean
For more than half a century.
They are happy with their families.

My husband is living in a nursing home
In Ottawa, not knowing what tomorrow will bring
For him or me. He does not have any responsibility
For anyone; he only knows what is good for himself.

After half a century, I count the many
Challenges I faced in many walks of life
Wearing many new shoes,
Discarding the old ones.

FERIAL IMAM HAQUE

I have the honor of being known to the world

As a scientist in the field of pure and applied chemistry
And also in the field of forensic science, specializing in
Developing new methods to reveal latent fingerprints
At many crime scenes.
I played many roles in the community
I am a daughter, sister, mother,
And wife in my family.

In Ottawa I keep my household
And lead a busy life. I stay busy and bold.
Our daughters are grown, are well educated,
Are busy with their own lives.
This is my story I have now told.

Desire to Live

For many decades I have been struggling to survive under a multitude of trying circumstances in the different phases of my life. My teenage dream to become a scientist was very difficult to accomplish. Yet I reached the first step to acquire my PhD degree in science in 1970.

My second step was to be recognized as a scientist in the scientific community through publication. I could not find a research laboratory to continue with my research work. That was a sad experience in my life as a woman in science. Still, I never stopped dreaming of applying my knowledge of science to the field of science and the community. I moved into the area of forensic science, having been inspired by other scientists about the urgent need to open the doors to this profession in Canada. My nascent mind and curiosity became intoxicated with the thought of finding ways to reveal evidence to solve crimes. Yes! It was done, and the method has been known to solve murder cases in Britain.

My story began in the summer of 1975 when I was lying on a hospital bed at Grace Hospital in Ottawa. To keep me alive, I needed intravenous saline and soluble nutrients in my bloodstream to rejuvenate my body functions. I gazed at each drop dripping into the tube and as it traveled through the needle into my bloodstream. With the progression of time, intravenous feeding rejuvenated my body. I looked around, realizing I was feeling stronger and better. Of course, other patients were still healthier than I was.

Many questions came to my mind. I sought to find reasons for how and why I should recover and resume my endeavors. Simple answers to my thoughts became crystal clear for two reasons:

- I was the mother of two daughters—a baby and a nine-year-old—who were helpless and could not survive without their mother.
- I had an earnest desire to continue my life as a scientist to add my contribution to the scientific world, however small it may be.

FERIAL IMAM HAQUE

I made many decisions in the sixties and seventies that got me to where I am today. I made my decisions then and became determined to recover and regain my strength to slowly proceed to fulfill my objectives.

I am thankful to God for putting things in order for my husband and girls—thanks to my small income—to keep things moving while I had a mobility impairment from 2006 to 2009. Of course I again paid a heavy price, that is, the deterioration of my health.

I could not forget my past and my hospital stays to recover, rejuvenate, and resume my duties to reach the goals I had set in my twenties, as follows:

- I love myself and shall be true to my words and work.
- I will be my own friend no matter what!
- I must keep moving on my chosen path to reach my goal.
- I must receive an education to acquire knowledge.

Life will come to an end, yet I must leave good deeds and memories behind. I must say farewell to the ones who have no time for me, and I will not hurt anyone.

Once I returned home after my gallbladder surgery I began to move around with much difficulty, taking care of the baby and household duties.

I was not satisfied with my life, so I began to explore ways to find appropriate women's support groups to rejuvenate and reactivate my mind so I could regain my physical strength and participate as an active member.

My decision in 1976 had to do with multiculturalism and science in Canada:

- I started part-time work at the University of Ottawa.
- I joined the Ottawa Women's Multicultural Conference in 1976.
- Upon the request of the Folk Arts Council, I joined as vice president.
- I served on the committee for Canada's birthday party, the Tulip Festival, and other summer festivals.

- I did research in forensic science, linking Ottawa University, the Royal Canadian Mounted Police, and National Research Council of Canada (NRC).

In 1983, my term work at Consumer Cooperate Affairs terminated. I was without any job and thus became lost in a sea of mysteries.

My decision in 1983 involved the following things:

- Publishing on topics including forensic science and community involvement through the Ottawa Board of Education, leading to political issues and concerns.
- Fund-raising for health charities.

My principles were based on creating local support groups for patients and their families, but only for small charities. I chose this because I'd had no support when I was confined to bed after my gallbladder surgery in 1975.

I earned two diplomas in writing by way of correspondence courses.

Songs That Inspire

Songs of all kinds
Calm our minds.
One childhood song
I used to sing in the school choir
At Strand-on-the-Green in London
In the early fifties

Makes me think of days
I was carefree, without any worry.
We sang in the choir
Songs that inspire.

Oh! Where are the songs
of my childhood,
Those when I would sing,

"Time, you old gypsy man.
Will you not stay?
Put up your caravan
Just for one day?"

It did not make much sense.
As a child I would ask, "Why?"
And why would I ask
the old gypsy man anyway

To put away his caravan and stay?
Why is, and how can, the gypsy man be
Like the time?
None of this made sense then.
Now I get a glimpse of what it means.
My way with maturity.

Bengali Songs

What about the songs
I loved to sing in Bengali?
Your words are such a beautiful
Gospel.
Your messages are
So inspiring.
Your songs take me
To another world
Full of pleasure and dreams.

What about the songs
The composer
Narrates to his lover with deep emotion
To express his passionate love?
Lyrics of his songs inspire me.

"I am the pleasure of
The foot bells of a dancer.
I sing the tunes she enjoys and
Interprets graciously in the
Rhythm and beat with her movement."
In response to my song I sing,

"Where is this beautiful gracious dancer?
You are my love as you inspire me.
You continue to dance
While I compose my lyrics
And keep singing to inspire you."

Magic of Hope

Ottawa is covered with snow
From December to the end of March.
Santa and his reindeer Rudolph, in the sleigh,
Visiting every chimney to drop off
Surprise gifts to children for another year.

Children are waiting for this special day,
Anxious to receive their presents and
Open them after rejoicing to celebrate.
They savor a turkey dinner on Christmas Day
With family and friends.

After dinner everyone gathers by the fireplace.
Sure, their hopes are high that they will enjoy their surprise gifts.
December 31 ends the year after Christmas,
Welcoming another New Year with food, drink,
Music, dancing, and fireworks.
What a wonderful way to end the year!

I Sing the Songs of My Life

Why do I wish to sing the songs of my life?
I have always wondered why my life was so different!
My dream of who I wanted to be as a respectable woman.
I did not know the rules of the world community,
But I craved for peace around me as a dreamer while
Traveling and stopping over to find a purpose in a certain country.
Conclusion: it is a privilege to learn, and to learn the many traditions.

I grew up in a family with centuries of aristocracy,
Family traditions within the limits of their rules.
I and my siblings grew up within the strict guidelines
Set by these rules and regulations.
Conclusion: it is part of my identity to be proud of living in society.

I never knew what it meant to have a father.
He could not bear the pain caused by his failing heart.
There was no magic cure and no miracle of medicinal art.
Peacefully, he said goodbye to his three daughters
And the wife he admired so fondly and loved.
My inference: God has the final say over our destiny.

Now I have grown up to be
Who I am, living in my adopted land.
I was running away from the war where I was born.
All I can recollect and say with pride is that
I am proud to be who I am today.
Conclusion: the life of an immigrant is not easy. Accept what you get!

I have many anecdotes of the obstacles that
obstructed my path on my way
To my goal in life, yet I survived and was able to move on.

Today, I audit my activities of survival and my progress
With family conflicts and the international battlefield.
Boldly like a warrior I stood steadfast to survive the war.
Conclusion: strive to bring peace wherever you go, learn to contribute
Without any question or conflict, and solicit harmony.

It made me stronger and wiser never to question any encounter
When we came to Ottawa, Ontario, in Canada.
I could sleep without any fear of human terror.
I could think with a mind uncluttered by fear.
I thought of how I could become a key player and devise ways
To earn a living so
We could build a new life with a new vision.
My conclusion and action: be a visionary person as a woman.

While drawing up the blueprint of my life, I experienced
Poverty, hunger pangs, shivering in the cold winter days
In Ottawa in the early seventies. Important variable elements
Played key roles in allowing me to jump the hurdle of poverty
— a vicious circle in society.
I began to remember the good deeds of men
who ventured to find new ideas.
They were the explorers or pioneers of the past to build humanity.
My conclusion: engage in the dignity of labor
and hard work wherever you are.

I have gained experience in the chemistry research laboratories in
Many cities—Ottawa, Canada; Glasgow,
Scotland; Atlanta, Georgia—
Not to mention that I grew up amid entrenched family traditions
And the societal limitations and expectations placed on women
Around the world in the past and today.

We enjoy the contributions and convictions of many
Dedicated and pioneering women who worked
for our claim to be a person.

I cherish the fruits of their toil and sacrifice for womanhood.
My inference: move on each day with dedication and perseverance to
Be proud of who women are and what we can achieve
As mothers, daughters, and
Lovers to create a peaceful family and society.

I recall the topics of
International Women's Week: the voice of women;
Health care (which includes medical science);
Chemistry, including the origin of medicinal
plants as gifts of nature; and
Education to enlighten a woman's life.
Women are caregivers and creators of society.
We are the rocks of society and the global community.
Women provide the inspiration to create
unusual memories and monuments:
Silver Cross Mothers, lovers (Taj Mahal), Joan of Arc,
Madam Curie's gift of radium (the x-ray).

Prelude to Chapter 5

In this chapter the author captures the extreme weather of the different places she has lived and where she grew up. Here she shows us through images and words the beauty of nature of Canada.

Chapter 5

Seasons

Just living is not enough …
One must have sunshine,
Freedom and a little flower.

—Hans Christian Andersen

New Year's Day

The clock strikes twelve.
I turn a new page
On the first day of January 2013
To welcome another new day.
I promise to record my experiences,
Good or bad, and the activities of each day!

Gone are the days and nights
Not worthy of remembering,
But I will not tear out those pages
Or even erase, cancel, or scribble on them.

At dawn in the morning sunshine
I am eager and ready
To welcome and celebrate
New Year's Day!

I am eager to write my plans and the blueprints
Of my hopes and dreams for the year.
My creations will be adventurous and wondrous,
So adults and children can enjoy the joys everywhere.

They will be grateful to our Creator for
Another New Year
To enjoy the snow and skiing, ice-skating,
Snow-shoeing, tobogganing, walking, and
Playing hockey.

Oh yes! The family together will make a snowman
Nice and tall, with raisins for eyes and a carrot for nose.
Of course, we'll have to do something about the
Snowman's mouth! Smart idea.

FERIAL IMAM HAQUE

Line the lips with red Smarties, but no teeth.

Then we'll wait for arrival of the spring
To wash away the melting slushy snow and sand.
Welcoming the birds flying from tree to tree
And the leaves covering the trees, flower buds will join
Wherever the eyes can capture the many shades of colors.
Trees will be many shades of green with green grass beneath.
Soon the many colors of flowers will enhance the beauty of the green.

Summer will bring rain and the warmth of sunshine.
The fruits and vegetables will grow and thrive.
Children will be happily playing everywhere, on the
School playground, in parks, and in backyards.
They will ride bikes, play basketball, and hike.

Soon the fall season will come to greet us.
We will see the crops ripen and change color
With another charming panorama of fall colors.
Everywhere people will be rushing and harvesting the crops
In the cool breeze and sunshine, surrounded by colorful trees
Like the artist capturing the beauty of nature on the canvas.

Parents will be busy shopping for school supplies.
The children will be getting ready for another school year
To learn from new teachers and play with old and new friends.
This is the way to learn and grow to be responsible citizens.

In October children will celebrate Halloween and
Enjoy dressing up, going door-to-door trick-or-treating
In the neighborhood on Halloween Night,
Collecting candies, chocolates, and chips for treats.

The month of November is sad and somber.
We remember on the eleventh day of November
The brave soldiers who have given their lives
For their country and our country, Canada.

Because of their patriotism in the line of duty,
We all enjoy nature's beauty and live in harmony.
Canada is so vast and diverse.
We cherish the peace among our people.
Sing along with the song:
"O Canada, we stand on thee."

The year ends in December
To welcome Santa and Rudolph and the other reindeer,
Bringing gifts for children and joy to their tiny hearts.
Enjoy Christmas dinner with turkey and plum pudding
The children open Christmas presents beside the fireplace.
What a wonderful way to end another snow-covered year!

Beauty of Nature

The gifts of nature surround us
With the sun peeking through the mountains,
Rejoicing in the musical voice of twittering birds.
Attracted by nature's little creatures like insects,
Ants, butterflies, bees, wasps, spiders, and more,
I see they are busy with their daily chores.
Bravely they are ready to face the daily challenges.

Looking around I see that the sky is sapphire blue.
Patches of white and gray create a great hue.
Wondering what the day will bring us today.
To unveil and face the secrets of the day.

I turn around to see green meadows
Covered with wildflowers and weeds,
Yellow dandelions, purple clover, bluebells.
"Wait," I say. "Are these the rainbow colors?"

I turn my eyes to my little flower garden,
Find that colorful butterflies are enjoying flying
From flower to flower, pollinating.
Bees are visiting the flowers, collecting pollen to make honey.
Spiders are hiding in search of poison to gather.
Ants are crawling at the roots of the plants,
Maybe to suck the juice from the roots.

Apple tree in the backyard and maple tree in the front garden

I think all creatures are busy working away
Just to complete the day's chores their own way.
I learn my lessons to motivate myself for the day
From the tiny creations of nature's teachers.
I say, "What a wonderful way to learn and earn.
I hope for the patience to wake up and greet a new day."

Oh, thank you, Lord, for the precious bestowal of
My vision, mobility, sense of smell, heart, and wisdom.
O to move around and enjoy learning from
Nature's creatures and teachers.

FERIAL IMAM HAQUE

This school of learning is free with new lessons.
What a wonderful and beautiful world we live in.

I welcome family, friends, and strangers
To join me. Rejoice in learning from nature's school.
No tuition or fees to bring our community together,
Living with people from many corners of the world.

April 21, 2017

Guess Who I Am

Maybe you think I am a little cat like
Grandma's cat who likes chasing her Tweety Bird.
She comes with her broom to chase the cat out.
I live with my family and friends in a single house.

The backyard is nicely enclosed in chain-link fence,
So I can't stray away and get into mischief.

I like running around in the backyard. It's pretty big.
Cedar hedges are on two sides. The feral cats like to visit.
Two neighbors are at the back. One of them stores garbage,
Which attracts rabbits, groundhogs, and sometimes skunks.
So the garbage side is covered with wooden boards.

I like chasing the many types of birds sitting in the apple tree
In the backyard in Ottawa, Ontario, Canada.
In the spring the apple tree is loaded with white blooms.
Near the house the magnolia tree is smiling with pink flowers.
I have a wonderful time chasing the cats, birds, and squirrels.

I am so lucky to enjoy the freedom to run around or sit on the porch,
I guess to sunbathe, or lie on the velvety
green grass in the summer sun.
Sometimes, I make too much noise when I am scared.
My master comes and scolds me because I disturb the older
Neighbors. I don't say much. I come in and go to my room.

I am lucky; I enjoy watching TV while sitting on the leather sofa.
Sometimes, I share the sofa with my master or my friend.
They like to rest their legs, lying on the sofa.
I like to mimic them and lie on the cushion or the blanket to rest.

FERIAL IMAM HAQUE

I do anything that makes me happy, climbing up the stairs,
Jumping up on the bay window, sleeping under the sofa.

I feel it is my responsibility to guard the house
When people or dogs are near our property, either from the inside
Or outside in the backyard.
On a sunny morning, I lie on the carpet and rest.
When I wake up, I go to my master and
Stare for attention and wag my tail.
I get my treat for being good for a while
And babysitting myself.

I will never forget some of the winter experiences and scares.
One night I jumped out the patio door, looking at the snow.
I waited on the porch, admiring the change created by the snow,
Thinking how to go down the stairs for my walk.

But I was scared by the sudden loud noise of snow falling
From the cedar hedges, breaking some branches.
I made a loud sound so my master would come and see.
She got up from the kitchen table and stood by me.
I was quiet and stopped, looking at her.

Winter ice storm in January 1998. Broken trees.

Then again that winter, we had lots of snow and fierce wind.
It was just a few days later when we heard a loud bang.
The sound woke us up at night, but soon it was gone.
I walked with my master around the house,
But there was nothing we could see, so we went back to sleep.

The next day our local TV news highlighted
The cause of the loud bang: a sudden drop in temperature.
The loud bang was called a "frost quake."
It kept children, adults, and our animal friends awake.

I enjoy going for a walk in the snow with my friend.
It's so nice to walk in the snow and breathe the fresh air,
But when we get home, I have to wipe my paws
To clean the salt and gravel stuck in between my toes.
I also like having my face washed every day.

Max on the sofa in 2005

Now can you guess who I am?
I am a dachshund. My parents came from Russia.

I and my nine siblings were born in Aylmer, Quebec.
I was sold to my friend for $700 and came to Ottawa.
She named me Max. I run to my friend whenever she calls.

The smell of food excites me so much that I jump and run,
Never giving up until I get what I want.
Once I ate raw chicken breast and landed in the veterinarian hospital
In Toronto. My friend had to send me to Ottawa
With her mother. I stayed in the hospital for a couple of nights,
Then I came home on Halloween Day and stayed with her.
I like her company! She still calls me Puppy when I am naughty.

11 Lillico Drive in the summer

This is my story in short.
I hope you enjoyed learning my activities of freedom while living
With my family and friends in Ottawa.
My postal address is 11 Lillico Drive.

Looking through My Patio Door

All I can see is white fluffy snow, so calm and serene.
The neighbors' green hedges are sprinkled with the same.
It is dull and gloomy out.
The wind is bitter cold.

Max, our dachshund, jumps out the patio door and
Waits on the porch, perhaps admiring the change and
Thinking how to go down the stairs for his walk.

Max in the snow at 11 Lillico Drive, winter 2005

Just a few days ago, we heard a loud bang.
The sound woke us up at night, but soon it was gone.
I walked around the house with Max guarding me,
But there was no change I could see.

The next day our local TV news highlighted
The cause of the loud bang: a sudden drop in temperature.
The loud bang was called a "frost quake."
It kept children, adults, and our animal friends awake.

All I say is that these are the blessing of Mother Nature!
What a wonderful way to begin the New Year.
Like always, wishing for a better and peaceful year,
I can only hope for a happy tomorrow and the day after.
Max and I make a good pair sharing our time together.

We wish everyone around us a happy New Year.
We welcome with great warmth the year 2015.
Hope will drive us through each day
To cope with the new challenges we face.

This is my story in short.
I hope you enjoyed hearing about my activities of freedom while living
With my family and friends in Ottawa.
My postal address is 11 Lillico Drive.

Images of Spring

March is here, so spring will be near.
March 20 is the spring equinox.
Then comes the first day of spring.
The days are getting longer,
So the days are getting brighter.

March brings hope and joyous memories.
March is such an interesting month
For women and families.
March 8 is a special day for women.
On March 12 daylight saving time begins.

March 14 is very special for the mathematician.
It is called Pi Day, symbolized by
the Greek letter π.
π = (the circumference of a circle) ÷ (the radius of a circle).
It has a value of 3.14159.

Anyhow, my daughter and I celebrate
Pi Day because she is a mathematician.
We make many pies of different kinds:
Apple crumble pie, pear pie, pecan pie,
Lemon pie, blueberry pie, meat pie, and what else?

What a thrill to shop for the ingredients after
Finding our favorite recipes for these pies.
First, she makes the dough for each kind.
Rolling begins. Next the filling goes in the pie crust.
I don't mind helping to make and bake
All these pies, taste them, and finally store them.

In Ottawa, spring does not arrive
Until the snow melts away and Jack Frost leaves.

FERIAL IMAM HAQUE

We all know that in Ottawa, Ontario, Canada,
If March comes in like a lion,
Then it goes out like a lamb.

But this year, 2017, March did not come in
Like a lion with a snowstorm,
So we have been experiencing a snowstorm
All throughout this month, with
Three to four feet of snow on our lawn.
What a serene look. Wherever my eyes go,
All I can see is fluffy white snow,
Which has very short life span.
With the warmth of the sunshine, it disappears.

I am mesmerized by nature's miracle.
As a chemist, I can see, touch, and admire
The three different phases of the molecule H_2O.
When it rains, it is the liquid phase of water.
When it snows, it is the solid phase. Ice is also solid.
The clouds are in the gaseous phase.

All I can say is, Let it rain and let it snow, but not
The rain that freezes and makes my life miserable.
Oh yes, an accumulation of fluffy snow is hard to clear,
Yet I don't mind that the snow is here.
The month of March welcomes all forms of water
To give us a sense of winter and then spring.

August 31, 2017

A Rainy Day

I tell myself that I am not made of sugar or
other water-soluble ingredients.
Sure, I won't dissolve in the rain and flow along in the rainwater.
I must go out to do my shopping for my food and drink
So I can eat and have the energy to go to school and learn.
I can then get a job and earn money to pay for my living expenses.

But I am strong and made of water-insoluble ingredients.
I have skin that covers my body parts: my feet, face, and head.
When I was a child, I learned that my head was most important.
I often wondered why, because it is covered with my black hair,
And my fingers tell me it is as hard as rock, so how can it crack?

As I grew older and read about my head and its contents,
I learned that actually it protects the brain,
which controls our activities.
"Oh!" I said. "So it is the home of all the mechanical parts of me!
These are made up of soft tissues connecting to blood vessels.
It is far too complicated for little old me."
I surrendered, resolving to learn and be happy and live in misery.

What about the skin? I wonder what it is made of. I take a shower to
Clean my body covered with dirt, and now I feel so good and fresh,
But I don't wash away with the water. Wow! My skin is better than
My raincoat, which my mummy and daddy
tell me to wear on a rainy day.
At the end of the school day, the teacher will tell us,
"Children, don't forget your raincoats! It is raining."
So I am happy with my story of a rainy day!

FERIAL IMAM HAQUE

August 22, 2017, 11:08 a.m.

Hailstorm in Ottawa

Today, I was greeted by a hailstorm.
I heard a tapping noise outside, and
I opened the door to the porch.
Oh, what did I see?
Like little pebbles,
It was translucent pellets of ice!
Did I wonder why?

Yes, I did wonder while standing on the porch,
Breathing fresh air, and gazing at the sky.
I wondered how clever must be the Creator of this
Transformation of water molecules into the
Solid phase and carrying them to the ground
With the liquid phase as the vehicle.
The mystical force of nature, the Creator.

Driving in the reverse gear, going back in memory to
My childhood days to dream and fictionalize
What I recall of my memories then, almost
Seven decades ago, to think and write about the
Memories of a child in her birth country.

Wild Canada Geese Are Leaving

The title sings the song of the wild geese honking to prepare for migration in the fall to escape the cold winter weather in Canada and the northern part of the United States. The geese migrate back to the north in the spring. Other wild animals also prepare for the winter. They will hibernate and then awake in the spring.

The most familiar and widely found wild geese in Canada have a majestic appearance with a black head and neck, white chinstrap, light tan to cream breast, and brown back,

The geese are family-oriented animals. With the advent of the spring, the mated pairs of geese raise their families. Usually they are chatty. Among family they are always vocal, as they are while on the ground, in the air, during feeding, when waking up in the morning, and before they sleep, so they love to chat.

Some vocalizations are unique to a family for purposes of identification and location. The honks can vary. It's just a goose's way of being part of the group and to add its own voice to those of the larger group. Some honks are to alert others to danger, food, of predators. The young goslings just go off with a jag of honking to express joy and excitement over their ability to fly with their friends and family.

Canada geese are well-known for their seasonal migrations. The migration of Canada geese begins in the fall, from September to early November. On their migration route, they have staging or resting areas where they join up with other geese. The early migrants spend less time at rest stops and go through migration much faster, whereas the geese migrating later usually spend more time at rest stops, usually on their return to the same nesting ground year after year. They nest to raise a family: the female geese lay eggs with their mates to teach the goslings to swim, feed, and fly each year.

Canada geese have a distinctive V-shaped flight formation, with an altitude of one kilometer (three thousand feet) for migration flight. The maximum flight ceiling of Canada geese is unknown, but they have been reported at nine kilometers (twenty-nine thousand feet).

Flying in the V formation has been the subject of study by researchers. The front position is rotated since flying in front consumes the most energy. Canada geese leave the winter grounds sooner than they leave their summer grounds.

While in migration flight, to keep track of one another in the fluid flock, the family members make a series of short honks. When arriving closer to staging areas, resting areas, or feeding areas, their honking picks up in tempo and there some additional, longer honks. This communication is to draw attention to other members in the flock and urge them to pay attention for a safe landing.

Like the Canada geese migration, we humans migrate south to escape the harsh winter in Canada. Of course, this seasonal migration depends on those who can afford to join the snowbird team migrations, which are of concern to US immigration, wildlife conservation, and economic authorities.

Prelude to Chapter 6

Having lived and pursued graduate studies in many countries, the author encountered many people in many roles. Her purpose here is to depict a few of her experiences in society.

Chapter 6

Human Nature

When the world says, "Give up," hope whispers, "Try it one more time."

Today's World

In today's global community
Let us pledge to live in harmony.
We are educated and connected to the world
With the blessings of high-tech, with media to
Communicate and hopefully to
Unite us together with words of value to
Show kindness and love to those
Who believe in and live with hate.
Why not change to bring peace
And learn to live in harmony
In the global community?

Our Creator created us to love and be loved, to
Be kind and be grateful for what we have.
We are blessed with nature's gifts to survive,
But when nature is angry, it brings natural calamities:
Thunderstorms, rain, blizzards, and forest fires.
These things hurt animals, human beings, and their dwellings.
Call for evacuation becomes a priority.
People realize their life savings and all their possessions
Are of no value in the escape from nature's fierce
Power of destruction and cruelty.
People seek for shelter in public places
And quench their thirst and satisfy their hunger
With drink and food given by kind people
And charitable groups within the community.

FERIAL IMAM HAQUE

I can't understand why we need to
Protest, hate, and act violently in anger to.
Destroying peace, killing and injuring innocent humans—
What are we trying to achieve and prove to people?
Citizens of the global community,
Let us bring love and rejuvenate our hearts.
Eliminate hate and bring back peace.
Let us live in harmony and sing of joy, love, and peace.

Voices

O! Echoes of those voices
Are resonating in my ears,
Giving me the jitters.
So many voices with so many views.
I'm bombarded with stories
Of their miserable lives,
Like bees buzzing in their hives.

"Stop those voices!"
I say. "And stay away."
Why waste the precious time of my old age
When I have slowed down to clear my way?

O how I want to get away and be free,
Putter away with my daily chores to see
Nature's beauty in the morning sunshine.
I want to enjoy the day working away,
Banking, paying bills, shopping,
Cooking, cleaning, and finishing my to-do list,
And then enjoy the evening to rest.

Turn off those voices and let me meditate
So that unwanted advice will fade away.
Then I will submerge myself in my work for the day
That must be done straightaway.
I'll be productive and smile away.

Those people are like orchids:
I want to keep them out of my sight
While I fight for my independence and rights and
Finish my work to keep my height.

FERIAL IMAM HAQUE

I can hear the orders from those voices.
Some are sane, and others are insane.
Turn off those voices to end the day
At sunset. Finish the chores
To rest and start a fresh day.

When the Doors Closed

The world is a strange place.
You never know whom to trust.
Perhaps because people are full of lust,
People see the world as they are.

I am not a writer or historian.
I am only a person.

Having survived the war, my wish and dream is to live
A peaceful life with new dreams.

Over the four and a half decades
I have felt hunger pangs.
I coped with rejection and pains,
Surviving the cruelty of people
Closing the doors.

I was perplexed because the reason
Was unknown to me.
I can only say that sooner or later
I will meet my Creator.

There are no questions to ask.
My time is occupied with many tasks.
How can I solve the jigsaw puzzle
To create my peaceful dream life?

No mercy, no forgiveness,
But words resonating.
How I have become so useless
Seeing how all doors are closing.

This is a life so unique that
No one can wish for it.
Life can't consist of only one-way traffic.
I wish for my afterlife to be terrific.

Time has come for me to say goodbye,
Wishing all those
Who have said, "Away you go," to
Find a place in the gutter and go.

I will bid farewell to the world.
I am proud to be who I am, living among those
Who hate me so much,
Closing all doors and such.

Federal Election 2015

October 19, 2015, is a day to remember.
We voted to bring change and were so eager.
It was a remarkable campaign after almost a decade,
Thanks to leaders and voters asking
To see a change.

Leaders of all the political parties
Voiced their vision and the platform of their party.

Unlike with other elections, I had no roles to play.
As DRO (deputy returning officer) for Election Canada,
I enjoyed following the election results on TV,
Anxiously waiting to see which party
Would form the new government to rule Canada.

The doors closed after twelve hours of voting.
Ballots were carefully counted.
Results were reported to Election Canada.
The results were posted in the media.

We were counting each second, waiting to see
What all the eligible voters had to say.
Thank you so much, journalists and the media, for
Keeping voters well-informed with full details
Of the election campaign 2015 in fulfillment of our wishes.

I agree with the critics voicing their views.
The leaders' debates to explain their vision—
You all had some good points to make.
So voters marked their ballots with confidence.
Now voters have chosen their prime minister
To form a majority government that will serve for four years.

Keeping my fingers crossed, I will begin my
Personal homework to reduce my deficit budget and
Keep abreast of the new financial economic budget created
By Canada's newly formed government.

By the time next election comes to our doorstep,
Each party will be ready to embark on
Another election campaign trail
To make Canada the best country on the global stage.
We the voters again will be doing our
Individual homework to participate
As active members to bring about change.

Remembering the 2015 election campaign
Supported by eligible grassroots voters
From the east coast to the west coast of Canada.
Voters were assured in all corners of Canada
That this change would make Canadians
Healthier and happier and ensure security and prosperity.

Many finer details were explained about our environment.
We are blessed with a clean and friendly ecosystem.
We learned how we will care for the animal kingdom
As well as for their human friends.

With my perception of science and society,
I appreciate the leaders' promised responsibility.

My vision as a chemist is that all parties have embarked
On the next phase of their evolution

Like the phase diagram of water.
With change in temperature and pressure,
Water molecules are shaped in three phases:
Liquid, gaseous, and solid—
Water, vapor, and ice.

Now the leaders are sitting in the House of Commons
To ensure Canadians will soon be living
On stable ground, not drifting
Like in the liquid phase of water or evaporating
In the gaseous phase, losing our identity,
But moving toward the solid phase
To crystallize into ice, taking many shapes
Depending on the container the party provides.

Any party, whether majority or minority,
Stands on a similar stage.
Time will tell their activities, small or big,
Each day to enact the change voters desired, such as
Better housing, higher income,
The eradication of poverty, increased security,
A safe shelter for women and children,
Better education for our children,
Better health care, and a friendlier community
To make Canada a peaceful country. Globally,

Canada's role has been peacekeeping.
We endeavor to continue this objectivity
In all walks of lives within the family and society,
Then reach out to the global community to lobby for peace.

Hoping for better and peaceful days ahead
To live in harmony in a country with a vast amount of space,
Blessed with an abundance of natural resources,
Each of us will be responsible for our own fate.

As a take-home examination for the next four years,
On a new page our daily living expenses
We will record each day
Until the next election in four or five years.
Hope to meet you at the polls.

Thanks for your time.

FERIAL IMAM HAQUE

Today Is Nine Eleven

Time has gone by fast,
Yet the grief still lasts.
Our hearts can't
Heal the scar of 9/11, which happened
A decade and a half ago.

All around the world
We mourn the unthinkable
Loss of lives in New York, the buildings
Crumbling down because of human error.

I and my colleagues
In the call center for the Kidney Foundation were
Working away, preparing for a
Fund-raising campaign
To bring comfort to patients.

Suddenly, we heard the radio news"
Terrorist attacks in the United States
Approximate number of lives lost,
Nearly three thousand, including twenty-four Canadians.
They were all innocent human beings.

My heart seemed to stop.
All I heard was why this happened.
We were worried about Canadians
Who were working in New York.
Casualty numbers were unknown.

The daughter of one of our colleagues worked there.
She lived close by,
But no contact could be made.
To relieve a mother's worry,
We all prayed for good news.

This horrifying memory
Took place fifteen years ago,
Yet the Western world can't forget—
Nor can the Canadians forget—
This solemn day.

Our heartfelt sympathy and support
Goes to the families and friends of
Those innocent people who lost their lives.
Many are still living with physical and emotional
Problems caused by the 9/11 attacks.

We honor the bravery and courage
Of those who responded on that day
And the days that followed.
As human beings, we honor the EMTs,
The firefighters, the police, and
All those who ran to help others,
Risking their own lives and many more realities.

On this sad day lets us say,
"Let no such destruction happen again
Anywhere in the world.
Let us find ways to achieve peace and
Strengthen ourselves to declare a day of unity."

FERIAL IMAM HAQUE

Unfinished Dreams

Dreams and hopes keep me hoping
Throughout the day and night.
I am a daydreamer, and I
Act on my dreams whenever possible.
My childhood dream was to discover something unknown
That would be good for us all.

Did it come true?

Still unfinished, I say,
But I have not given up.
I am on the search to find new ways,
To find new paths,
To achieve my childhood dreams,
To reach my pot of gold.

Among the many sudden changes in my life,
The unexpected liberation of Bangladesh,
Creating a new country on the world map,
Compelled me to search for a new address
On the world map for a new beginning.

Now I am a proud Canadian,
Struggling alone at my old age.

I audit my contribution as a scientist
To find out my identity, and my contributions
To the people around in the community.

I ask, "Who am I today?"

A scientist, a chemist, or a forensic scientist.
An activist or an artist or

A citizen of the global community.
I cannot forget the memories
Of my brief or long stay
In many of the places on the world map.

During my travels,
I have had many life experiences
In the classroom, in the society, and in the family,
All jumbled up.
But I say the key is to be a good person.
Wherever I may stay, I will create my home
The way I want it to be so that I am comfortable.

This is the story of my life
And my unfinished dreams.

You can search me on the internet as
Ferial Haque a Chemist
Ferial Haque a Scientist
Ferial Haque's Research Works -researchgate.net
Ferial Haque's Research Works – University of Ottawa & other places

This is the story of my *unfinished dreams*!

Prelude to Chapter 7

Here the author walks us through her rough journey as a professional immigrant woman juggling the roles of mother and wife while trying to earn a living. In her many years as a Canadian immigrant, she has faced some bitter truths and encountered some naked facts that have left many scars in her mind. With persistence, hard work, and long hours she has partially achieved her goals, which she depicts in "Unfinished Dreams."

Chapter 7

New Canadian

Learn from yesterday, live for today, hope for tomorrow.
The important thing is not to stop asking questions.

—Albert Einstein

A New Beginning

I am a proud Canadian
Although my birthplace
Is in a faraway land
That evolved from undivided
Bengal under British rule
To East Pakistan on August 14, 1947/
Then, on December 16, 1971,
A new nation called Bangladesh
Was born.

I was exhausted during the turmoil of
The liberation movement of Bangladesh,
Always being on the road to
Save my life, with my child
Under the protection of my mother and
Her siblings—my aunt and uncle—
In Dhaka, the capital of Bangladesh.

Then came the choice of
Starting a new life
In another country.

It seemed Ottawa
Attracted us like it was a magnet and
We were the iron filings.

Returning to Ottawa
Without any source of income
Was not a pleasant memory.

Ottawa had changed from
September 1963 to July 1972.

FERIAL IMAM HAQUE

Donations of household goods
Poured in from friends and well-wishers.
My spirits were lifted by their kindness.
My creative juices were brewing
To begin my new journey
On an unknown road.

With many well-wishers,
I managed to grasp the concept
Of survival and existence.

Our basic need was to have a roof over our heads
So we could eat, rest, and work to earn a living.

Selling my knowledge and
Skills in science and culture,

I marched along in different walks of life to
Contribute to society at large,
To know and be known
In my world in Ottawa.

I pause to revisit my memory bank to
Search for my skills.
Oh! I thought back then,
I can sew, clean, cook.

My dream was to enrich the
Way of life in Ottawa with
A taste of multiculturalism.

Yes! My dreams have come true,
With diversity of culture,
Language, dress, food, music, and art.

Somerset Street West and Preston Street
House many ethnic shops and restaurants.
We all know Chinatown and Little Italy.

Being on Welfare

Learning to Survive
Landing at Montreal Airport on July 21, 1972
With my daughter and husband,
I did not know what our fate would be

Because

I wanted to sleep, rest, and live,
Having survived the liberation movement of Bangladesh.
We came to Ottawa to make our home.

We were greeted by my friends from the sixties.
Our temporary place of residence was at 423 Sunnyside Avenue,
Where I'd stayed as roomer when a student at Carleton.

I slept for many hours to catch up after my sleepless nights,
Being on the run from place to place, helplessly in fear.

My little daughter woke me up late afternoon.

Our fate was so clear upon returning from
Manpower and Immigration
The government agreed to support us,
placing us on welfare temporarily.

Then I was faced with another high hurdle to jump,
Faced with a series of hard life decisions.

I was on the phone calling to find a place to live.
Numbers were listed under ads for housing in the *Ottawa Citizen*.
It was more difficult to find an apartment with children.
Our decision was to rent a house and share with students.

FERIAL IMAM HAQUE

My only demand was that we rent to foreign graduate students
So that was the case.
We set out for the Department of Housing at Carleton
To place our ad for foreign student tenants.

Our search to find a house was successful on September 1, 1972.
I got phone calls from students,
But they wanted meals included with the room, what with
Being away from home for the first time.
There were no Indian restaurants in Ottawa then.

My memory takes me back to September 1963,
When I first came to join my husband.

Of course, I enjoyed Chinese food at Cathy House and Ho Ho
So, I thought and said, "You can have meals with us,
Whatever we eat."

The deal was made, and I thanked God for the source of income.
This was successful for a year, and then the student left Ottawa.

But other students accepted the same offer.
This continued for another five years.

Meanwhile, I was doing part-time research at Carleton and
demonstrating chemistry labs.
My husband was in the same situation.

But
Men with families had a few more points in their favor,
Whereas I was caught up in the circle of gender issues
As a professional immigrant woman.

A Tale of Tragedy

My story of "A Tale of Tragedy" is influenced by two concepts I have held so dear in my heart: International Women's Day and women's rights in our global society. So many tragic stories of victims of war are documented in the media. Writers, poets, political figures, and thinkers have given their many interpretations of tragedy in novels, stories, and speeches. The twenty-first century is very different from the twentieth century. I find that communication, technology, and social values are so different now from six decades ago. Today's world is very fast-paced with digital technology, and the world over is influenced by pop culture.

"A Tale of Tragedy" is the story of a woman who was born seven decades ago in a land under British rule known as British India. In this land there arose many great people like Rabindranath Tagore, who won the Nobel Prize for Literature; scientists like S. N. Bose, who was one of the originators of the Bose–Einstein theory; Mother Teresa; and Mahatma Gandhi—and many more.

The woman, the author, was born in the Chakma raja's residence situated atop a hill in Chittagong during World War II in the early forties. Her parents were well educated and came from aristocratic families. Her father loved her dearly and thought the world of her. Sadly, she lost her father when she was an infant. However, her childhood was imprinted with his scientific ideas, his having been a student of S. N. Bose. Her dream was that she would be a scientist like her father.

She had a tough life along the way of accomplishing what she had set out to contribute to science in the four decades of her life. There were trials and tribulations along her journey of life. She faced the challenges, through each step juggling many responsibilities as a wife, a mother, a student, and a researcher.

Her first experience with sadness was not being accepted by the rural culture of her country. Her determination in her youth and continued persistence led her to achieve her goal.

In January 1968 she left the sad experiences behind in Canada and moved to the United Kingdom. This led her to the new path she'd

FERIAL IMAM HAQUE

dreamed of creating: crystallizing her knowledge and skills in science. She wrote her PhD dissertation and documented her creations for other scientists so they could have the pleasure of reading them and exploring her efforts to benefit humanity.

In 1972 she, along with her husband and daughter, decided to return to Canada to begin a new life. She knew they would be moving into another little box and that she would bounce within its four walls. But she was like the blacksmith hammering on molten iron to give shape to a new structure, a new lifestyle.

Finally, she halted her quest for science to settle in her new home in Ottawa. She welcomed technologists and scientists who were eager to collect further research findings to complete the draft for publication. Her request was that she would be the primary author of any publications. Many research papers were published in the *International Journal of Forensic Science*, the *Canadian Journal of Forensic Science*, *Canadian Police Magazine*, and the *Forensic Newsletter*. She is now living in her home at 11 Lillico Drive, where her children visit her at their convenience.

A Home

Home sweet home.
A home is a place full of dreams,
Where we rest, eat, and sleep.
We nurture our dreams to create.

My dream is to create a home
Where I and my children
Have the freedom to grow and thrive
With bountiful wishes and love.

The question is, how?
No jobs, no money.
"Oh!" I say
"How can I buy a home?"
Yet I did not give up.

Being an immigrant and a woman
Did not help matters.
I was faced with so many barriers
While walking on the path to the unknown.

Having survived the battlefield,
I wanted to find a space in a country
To live in peace with dignity,
But where is that space to stand and hold?

I was young and naive about social issues.
My husband's job was not permanent.
How could I tell him about my wishes?
Yet together we would need to create
A place to live with our child.

Ferial Imam Haque

I dreamed of a childhood story in England with the characters
Noddy and Big Ears, written by Enid Blyton.
Big Ears would pick up useful stuff
Every garbage day for Noddy's house.

Soon we were blessed with the kindness of friends
And help from the government of Canada
To set up our new home in Ottawa.
So, we rented a house from our Italian landlord.
The address: 238 Cambridge Street North, Ottawa.

Friends gave us their excess pots and pans,
Dishes, and utensils.
I remember going to a department store
Known as "Beamish" on Bank Street,
Where we got our winter clothing, bedsheets,
Pillows, pillowcases, bedcovers, and blankets.
I remember it was all free—no cost.
It was gift from the Canadian government.

Our next stop was at Neighborhood Services.
Bus #2 took us to the store on Wellington Street.
We all enjoyed picking spoons, knives & forks out the household stuff
And selecting essential furniture for the house.
We had no cash money, so everything was free!

My husband was entitled to an allowance for his dependents
As well as the basic rent for the house.
We decided to rent out a room to a foreign student.
We were both actively searching for jobs.
I got a part-time teaching assistantship at
Carleton University and Ottawa University.
My husband got a similar offer from Ottawa University.

After the academic year ended, we were both unemployed and
Living on unemployment insurance benefits.
Rent from the boarder helped to pay the bills and buy food.
Yet with renewed hope, we were again searching for jobs.
Hopefully soon we would be able to save money for our own home—
A plan stored in my mind—and not give up too soon.

FERIAL IMAM HAQUE

Prelude to Chapter 8

In this chapter are depicted the special days in life and the reason why we should celebrate to remember these days.

Chapter 8

Special Days

Each day is a special day and is another chance to live, to love, to try to do our best.

—Rani Italy

Father's Day 2015

Father's Day is on Sunday, June 21.
Father! Memories of you are fresh in my heart.
I don't know how long the pain will last.
I pray you can sleep without pain and rest in peace.

I was a baby when you were living,
So you live only in my memory.
You are a creation of my imagination only,
Inspired by the praises of family, your colleagues,
Students, and professors, and the support staff
Of the Department of Physics
At the University of Dhaka, Bangladesh.

I have always been so proud of you
And adored your intelligence and wisdom.
Thank you for choosing Mother as your wife.
She was beautiful and intelligent
And graduated with a BA with honors in philosophy
From Calcutta University, British India.
Her family was wealthy and well-known in British India.

Thank you for ensuring mother was financially secure.
Because of your life insurance, we traveled
With mother wherever she went.
She traveled to London, England, in 1950
As an MA student in philosophy with a scholarship.
So, we three sisters tagged along with her.
Even today, I remember the carefree days in London.
We enjoyed playing with friends at school.

And thank you for your wisdom.
You have sown the seed to acquire knowledge,
So not only Mother but also we three sisters

Ferial Imam Haque

Have pursued education to attain professional status
In the global society.
Our children have also followed in our footsteps
To become scientists, educationists, and physicians
And have careers in business.

Your praises have set a legacy not only in the family
But also among your students and their families.
I have my own personal story of being inspired by you
As a scientist, educationist, and researcher.
You made a great impression on my mind when I was small.
This has always motivated me in my difficult times,
Whether I was lying in a hospital bed in my country, or abroad,
Or in the chemistry research lab.

When I was a little girl, my aunt, mother's sister,
Would often tell me the stories of your love for me.
Even during the last years of your life, you would
Pick me up and say, "You are my Madonna."
You would brush my hair and comfort me when I cried.
In your memory, I still part my hair the way you did.
My complexion is like yours and not like Mother's,
But I did not care, as I wanted to be wise like you.
I used to read your handwritten notes and
Admire your penmanship and the diagrams.

When it was time to choose our career paths,
We three sisters followed in your footsteps
To acquire knowledge and be good students.
My older sister chose medicine,
My younger sister chose physics, and I chose chemistry.

I was accepted by the faculty of science at the
University of Dhaka, East Pakistan, now Bangladesh.
We must be scientists and follow your legacy.
I graduated with a BSc honors degree in chemistry.

I did not stop there but continued
Graduate studies abroad to be awarded with a PhD.
I pursued further research to contribute to the field of science.
My interests were in applied science and society.
Internationally my contributions are in forensic science.
My research findings have attracted attention
In forensic laboratories by researchers and technologists.
I provided the technical information they needed.

Sometimes, I feel so gratified with my achievements.
I always was so proud of your academic achievements
And your MSc thesis supervisor, Professor S. N. Bose,
Connecting us to the Bose–Einstein theory.
This makes me realize the world is so small.
Someone in your field will notice your contributions,
However big or small.
Researchers always require a topic to begin creation.
We are never satisfied with our findings,
So our search for the truth will continue.

Mother's Day 2014

Today is May 11, 2014.
This Sunday is so special.
Why?
Because in Canada
It is Mother's Day!

My mother is no longer in this world,
So I cannot send greetings of love.
She is sleeping in her final resting place
In another country, a graveyard
So far away!

All I can say is, I love you and miss you,
But I am happy that you are resting in *peace*.
I suppose our children will think of all mothers
Wherever they are and whatever they are busy doing.
We love our children whether they have time for us or not.

We are mothers and daughters.
We know the pain of being a mother.
We nurtured our children as best we could
To be good and kind citizens
Of the global community.
Today as mothers we remember
Rocking the cradles, caring in every way we could.
Now we are waiting to see the results,
How well they remember their mothers!
Best wishes to all caring mothers.
Thanks to the fathers for their support
In standing by our sides
In good times or bad times.

We can't forget that
Today is Mother's Day in Canada.

Mother's Day in Britain

Sunday, March 15, 2015, is a day of celebration
On the other side of the Atlantic Ocean.
The vast waters have not washed away.
My memories of London, England, in 1950–1952

Sweet are my memories of then.
Carefree, no worries,
Under my mother's umbrella of care,
Playing, learning at school.
Spending time with my two sisters.

I adored Mother as she juggled many diverse duties,
Being a postgraduate student in philosophy
At the University College, London, England.
Her principles of caring for her daughters
So different from others'
Because she was a widow in her twenties.

Mother as a master's student in philosophy at
Dhaka University, Bangladesh, 1946

FERIAL IMAM HAQUE

All I can say is, Thank you, Mother.
Because of your sacrifice
I am who I am today with so many ideas,
Having grown up in a faraway place,
Ottawa, Ontario, the capital of Canada,
With changing colorful seasonal weather.

Happy Mother's Day
In memory of my mother.

Mother's Day in England

Dear Sister, I wish you good health
On Mother's Day in Gillingham,
Sunday, March 15, 2015.
Enjoy it with my brother-in-law and my nephew
At lunchtime with a
Delicious mouthwatering menu!

On Mother's Day 2015 your experiences and narrative
Of embarking on motherhood is fascinating.
As you say, in the third week of March 1963,
Being alone in Oxford, there dawned on you
The blessings of motherhood!
Yet you were jobless in a strange country
So far away.

You had courage, confidence, and optimism,
Knowing your path was paved,
Only to step forward to achieve progress
Without any return to welcome motherhood.
Your trust in God gave you strength
To walk to the end of this unknown path
To come to where you are today.

Thank you for sharing your
Courageous experiences more than
Half a century ago,
Giving your wisdom to your sister
To be focused on self-development,
Using every opportunity to choose
Desirable items for comfort and health.

Thank you for your gifts of
Pounds, wisdom, and love

To celebrate Mother's Day in England,
My childhood land in the early fifties.

To close my story of
Mother's Day on
Sunday, March 15, 2015, in
Gillingham, England.
I'll wish you a happy Mother's Day.
Enjoy it with your loved ones!

Be My Valentine

On the fourteenth day of February,
Will you
Be my valentine?

Young and old
All over the world
Are in deep thought over
How to express their love
To their loved ones—
Parents, siblings, children, wife,
Friends, and neighbors.

We are rushing to the stores
To buy gifts for our loved ones.
In front of the flower shop
The sign reads,
"I love you!
Say it with flowers."

We all know this saying:
"Roses are red, violets are blue.
The honey is sweet, and so are you.
Thou art my love, and I am thine;
I drew thee to be my Valentine:
The lot was cast and then I drew,
And fortune said it should be you."

In today's high-tech world,
We are constantly chattering
With people we *love* or not
On an iPhone, a BlackBerry, a cell phone,

The internet, the landline telephone, or some other device.

The chemistry of love is complex.
Simply one can say it is
Passionate and compassionate love
Or
Love or lust.
This is triggered by a chemical
Known as dopamine.
In real life, an imbalance of dopamine
Is the cause of neurological disease,
Leading to marriage breakdown,
Divorce, and many unacceptable acts
Committed by people in today's world.
Will you be my valentine?

Valentine's Day

On February 14, 2015,
A day so especial in my life, I am
Searching for ways to say,
"Will you be my valentine?"

For the past half-century
I've made this day, one to celebrate
With cards, candies, and chocolates,
Rejoicing in the expressions of love.

I am sending messages of appreciation
Across the country, across the world, and at home
Just to say, "I appreciate your kindness.
Thank you for your support for me."

Yes,
Wherever I go and look around, I see
Messages of Valentine's Day everywhere
Decorated in different shades of red.
Boxes of chocolates, candies, gifts, cards,
All anxiously waiting for a loving person
To take me home and give to their loved one, saying, "Be my friend.
I will sincerely love you forever!"

Flower boutiques are splashed with colors,
So many varieties of roses, violets, daisies,
Ready to symbolize the message of the day:
"I love you. Be my valentine today!"

Often I was amazed by the garden of tulips
During the Tulip Festival in Ottawa.
The story behind this annual celebration is that it was begun
To celebrate the birth of Princess Margaret

At the Ottawa Civic Hospital during World War II.

Queen Juliana and the Dutch royal family send
Tulip bulbs every year for the Canadian Tulip Festival,
The world's largest tulip festival. It takes place each May
Here in Ottawa, Ontario.

My daughter and I during the Tulip Festival, 1981

So many tourists are among the crowd
Enjoying the beauty of tulips in the vast area
Overlooking the calm and quiet Dow's Lake.
At the end of the driveway beside some tulip beds,
Tourists are capturing their memories in pictures.

The Sound of Music, a live performance. Food stalls,
Restaurants, gift boutiques, and an information booth,
Are ready and eager to help the tourists.
What a party we host each May in Ottawa,
Canada's capital, with purple tulips included, a sign of royalty.

A gift of a red tulip in Persia symbolizes the
Expression of love. The black center of the tulip
Represents the lover's heart.
"I love you with my heart!"

My belated Valentine's message
For 2015 is to say,
With Tulip in many hues and colors and scents
To admire until another year,
Happy Valentine's Day wherever you are.

Sweet Pea Flowers

On the fourteenth day of February 2014,
I would love to say
I love you
With sweet pea flowers.
Will you be my valentine?

We know the story of love
And expressing it with red roses:
"Roses are red, violets are blue.
Sugar is sweet, and so are you."

But do we know the story of
How to say "I love you" with sweet pea flowers?

Sweet pea flowers are beautiful and have a sweet fragrance.
White, pink, red, violet, or purple,
They are reminiscent of butterflies in their shape.
They are borne singly or appear in clusters of two to four.
The fruit is a hairy pod about two inches (five centimeters) long.
Hundreds of varieties of the sweet pea plant exist.
Was this subject of any importance for genetic experimenters?
It was two scientists in the nineteenth century,
Reginald Crandall Punnett and William Bateson.

So, it must be important in science.
Does the pea have a popular scientific name?
Yes, chemists love the word *pea*.
PEA's chemical name is phenylethylamine,
As shown below:

Phenylethlyamine (PEA)

This is an amine that naturally occurs in the brain.
PEA is also found in some foods like chocolate.
We can say "I love you" with chocolates too!

The stores are decorated with many varieties of chocolates
Packed in boxes that are red, pink, or a combination of colors,
In all shapes and sizes, waiting to be picked up
And go home with you to meet your valentine.

Why is PEA so important?
Because PEA stimulates our romantic chemicals.
Much like an amphetamine,
It is responsible for releasing norepinephrine and dopamine.
These chemicals are found in your body when you are falling in love.
They are responsible for the head-over-heels, elated feeling of love.

On Valentine's Day
Let us say
We love everyone in the world.
Let us *hope* for
Peace and love!
And let us say with sweet pea flowers that
We love the world
On the fourteenth day of February 2014
From Ottawa, Canada's capital.

FERIAL IMAM HAQUE

Sisters So Sweet

Sisters, you are
So sweet and dear,
But someone
Is closing our door.

As Mother taught us,
We must always
Stand by each other
In happy and sad times.

We were separated
About half a century ago.
We grew up to be so different,
Living in two countries
Separated by a body of water so vast

Called the Atlantic Ocean.
You live on the east coast
In England.
I grew up on the west coast,
Which is known to all as being Canada's capital,
Ottawa, Ontario.

Three sisters at Ruquayyah Hall, 1962

Left to right: Older sister, younger sister, and the author

Yet we are bound
By the magic of love
So strong. And Mother's teaching
Has kept our hopes burning
Deep in our hearts.

It is our responsibility
To keep the flames of *hope*
Emitting the light
So we can follow Mother's legacy.

On Saint Valentine's Day
May we join together as sisters and
Send our love to
Our global community,
Saying loud and clear,
"Happy Valentine's Day!"

FERIAL IMAM HAQUE

April 8, 2017

Easter in Ottawa

Easter always brings hope to my heart.
It awakens me to dream of sunshine, longer days, the
Warmth of a gentle spring breeze, birds flapping their wings,
New leaves covering the bare trees. Below the grass is looking green.
People young and old, including children, are
coming to enjoy the gift of nature.

Easter reminds me of my childhood days
In the fifties, in a country that is so far away.
Yet the memories are so clear with no fear,
As Easter is a time of hope and faith so dear.
A child's mind is free of worries,
Hoping for miracles to happen anytime.

This land is London, England,
A country where I remember hearing the reminisces
Of soldiers from World War II and World War I.
Canadian soldiers were so bold and brave.
Today the world remembers the sacrifice the soldiers made
To protect and liberate Vimy Ridge
From the German soldiers a century ago.

At my childhood school, Strand-on-the-Green in London,
We celebrated the theme of Easter with
Songs, gifts, and stories of Jesus Christ and his sacrifice.
Our innocent minds were touched by these stories,
But I always waited to see miracles of little chicks hatching
With a bright lemon-yellow color, flapping their wings.

I wondered why chocolate Easter bunnies
Were sold everywhere and children loved to eat them.

I could not wait to open my wrapped-up bunny and taste it!
As the years went by and it came to be my turn to buy the best
Chocolate bunnies, I wrapped them up for my children
And their friends in Ottawa. This was in the seventies and eighties.

Easter is a time to make sure I see and know
The true meaning of my family and children.
Wise minds have expressed their views about
Family, love, responsibility as parents, and a home.

I see and realize children are not the property of parents.
Children are people who need love, care, and education to
Face the day-to-day challenges their parents encounter
And to survive another day. Be thankful for what you have.
Children grow up and embark on their personal journeys.
Today my hope and love for my family and friends
Seems to have another dimension with inner meaning:
Love, hope, sacrifice, and patience to embrace
Today's world!

FERIAL IMAM HAQUE

Prelude to Chapter 9

Here the author emphasizes the importance of the birthdays of living beings and of the land that she lives in. Canada is a land of immigrants from many corners of the globe. Canadians have a rich cultural heritage and diversity of mind. They are different from one another, but their common goal is to live in harmony in one country to bring about *peace* and *harmony*. Canadian soldiers are well-known as peacekeepers around the world.

Chapter 9

Birthdays

Life is a journey. Enjoy every mile.

Canada's Birthday, 1976

I remember 1976 was a turning point
In my life, a time when I came to learn about
People's nature, as I saw their other side—
Not their head but their tail!

I proudly accepted the invitation to
Organize an Indian dance by two little girls
On the main stage at Vincent Massey Park
To represent East Indian culture, music, and dance.

It became my responsibility to write a short description
Of the theme and narrate on the stage
At Vincent Massey Park in Ottawa, Canada's capital.
It is a well-known Bengali folk song that you can hear
Everyone humming and singing everywhere
from the street to the stage.
The famous folk singer Abbasuddin Ahmed sang the song:

"The strong heat of sunrays scorches mercilessly
The fruits, flowers, crops, and nature.
The Bengali peasant sings, praying for rain:
'Oh God, give us rain to quench the thirst of
The dried-up earth, lakes, and rivers,
And end the suffering of thirsty and dehydrated humanity.
God give us clouds, water. Give us shelter, O dear one.'"

At the close of the evening's multicultural performance
Held at Mooney's Bay Stage with the Trinidad Steel Band
And including folk dances from around the world,
We served thousands of cupcakes to children and adults.
A huge Dummy Cake was donated by Morrison and Lamothe.

Beautifully decorated, it was standing on a table nearby.
Written on it was
"Happy birthday, Canada!"
We were tired, but we did not give up until the end of
Canada's birthday celebration, at which time we headed toward home,
Singing, "Happy birthday Canada, and good night.
Until next year!"

February 15, 2018

Mother's Ninetieth Birthday

December 2007, I traveled to
My birth country, where you still lived,
To join the crowed to attend
A special celebration of your birthday.

I was wheelchair-bound because I'd fallen
And torn the ligaments of my left knee.
Confined to bed for almost a year,
I could not stand to be away
From you on such a special day in your life,
Your ninetieth birthday celebration.
I wanted to say a few words on this occasion.

Paying tribute to Ma on her ninetieth birthday, December 2007

I wondered then how you'd managed to live
Alone those ninety years, being dependent
On your support groups, your caregivers.

Ferial Imam Haque

Everyone sang the song of your good deeds,
Praised you in their chosen words, and
Paid their respects in many ways.

"Oh!" I said. "What will I say to show my gratitude?"
I stood at the lectern and found a few words
So I could tell the audience what I felt was true:
How you walked through the rough and tough
Days of your life with your three infant daughters,

Your achievements in life as a student of philosophy,
Traveling to study in London, England, with your daughters
In 1950, crossing seas and oceans and flying to Karachi
To board the huge ocean-bound ship that sailed for many days.
You safely arrived in England, achieved your goal,
Then returned home with honor and glory.
Your new journey in life began with much
Turmoil and triumph, but you never lost sight of
Creating a solid foundation for your daughters.
You had set the blueprint for their future.
They followed the instructions you gave them
To create their individual identities in faraway lands.

Meanwhile, you nurtured your interests,
Writing your autobiography, writing about social
Concerns for women and about children's education.
You wrote about other special occasions such
as International Women's Day,
Children's Day, and the Senior Women's Group, among many others.

You had a few sad memories from episodes in your life
That you never came to terms with.
Being a widow at such a young age, twenty-five years,
You were labeled as inauspicious, and that defined your status.
In society you were seen as a second-class citizen because
You were not the mother of a son.

My heart aches to read the words when you write of
These social taboos you could never accept.
You concluded by saying that as a student of philosophy,
You accepted the harsh reality of the cruel world.
Yet you wanted the liberty to establish your identity.
I did realize your wishes and left your legacy in the
Professor Akhtar Imam Foundation at Prioyprangon,
3 Shegun Bagicha, Dhaka, Bangladesh.

Your birth centenary was celebrated
With many speeches by respected citizens of Dhaka
For many days.

I would say what a wonderful dream you had.
Your youngest daughter has dedicated her life to creating
A memorable structure where your students and
Followers unite to sing your praises.
Hopefully, these memories will remain ever fresh
In the minds of the citizens of Bangladesh!

Ferial Imam Haque's
Seventy-Fifth Birthday

June is the month that changed my life.
I realized in my youth that in order
To be loved by others, I need to love myself.
I am gratified and love myself
Because whatever choices I've made,
They were the right ones, made for self-love.
Now after many decades,
I say I was at the right place.
Today I accept that it was self-trust.

Because of my self-trust and self-love,
I decided to change my identity
From Mrs., as they say,
To
Dr., to join the group who are thinkers.
In my youth I admired the brains
Who contributed to science and people's lives.
This amazed my innocent mind,
Drew me closer to nurture my intellectual love.
In June 1970 I was honored
By Strathclyde University and awarded
The title PhD, to be known as
Dr. Ferial Imam Haque.
This I call achievement!

As I began to learn and add to my knowledge,
I saw how it offended others.
I tried to enforce myself to change them,
But my efforts were in vain.
As I discovered, people were not ready.
Now I see that the young me was that person.

Today I thank myself. It is called letting go.

When I started learning and loving myself,
I accepted my emotional pain and grief.
I grew stronger to bravely face the truth myself.
Now I know: it is called authentically being.

Because I began to trust and love myself,
I stopped wanting to be like any another person.
I continued to accept everything surrounding me.
Now I realize: it's called maturity.

When I started to trust and love myself,
I walked toward my goal with confidence and sincerity.
I stopped sketching and drafting new projects.
Today I only do what is essential for me and my family.
I do what I love, and I do it well,
In my own way, in order to be content. And my heart is full.
I do things at my pace and laugh
If my heart does not want to be so high.
Now I know: it's honesty.

When I started trusting and loving myself,
It was then I could discover what was not healthy for me,
From circumstances, to things, to people, to foods,
And all other things that pulled me down and depressed me.
I thought it was called "healthy egoism."
Today I know: it's called self-love.

When I started loving myself for my wisdom,
I did not always want to be right.
Only then did I become less wrong.
Now, I realize: it's called humility.

When I started loving myself,
I no longer wanted to lead my past life.
So I would not worry about my future.

FERIAL IMAM HAQUE

Now, with my wisdom, I live in the present.
I live each day as I see it happening each moment.
I call it consciousness.

Now that I am confident of myself,
I recognize that my thinking
May not be right and may make me miserable.
When I seek for my heart's force,
I see my mind has an important partner.
Today I call this connection heart wisdom.

So now I know we do not need further discussion.
Conflicts and problems with myself and others
Are the way of life. We live and learn each day
To create a new world.
Today I know: *this is life!*

A Special Day, June 21, 2018

It is a special day. "Why?" I asked.
"Because," Mother said,
"You were born today many decades ago!"
I enjoyed celebrating my birthdays,
I suppose, and I always will.

What a surprise! I got a bouquet of red roses
On my Facebook page from a Facebook friend,
Wishing me happiness and good things.
I dream that more good hearts will become my friends.

June 21 is the first day of summer.
I like to feel warmth of the summer breeze,
Enjoy the songs of birds perched on trees.
They will fly from place to place and sing,
But the melodies will linger.

June 21, 1970, was the Summer Convocation of
Strathclyde University in Glasgow—a special day for me.
I was honored with a diploma for my doctor of philosophy degree,
Changing my salutation to Dr. Ferial Imam Haque.

Today is also important for remembering kidney cancer.
To commemorate the day, we wear green lipstick.
I remember that I spent hours every year participating
In Celebration of Life and organ donation in Ottawa and
Decided to be captured in the Green Ribbon picture.

Today, June 21, 2018, is National Indigenous Peoples Day.
In Canada we celebrate the unique heritage and diverse cultures of
The First Nations, Inuit, and Métis peoples,
and their tireless efforts and
Tremendous contributions to this country, our Canada.

I am proud to be a Canadian, to remember the many special days: Canada Day, Remembrance Day, Refugee Day, Women's Day, Children's Day, Mother's Day, Father's Day, International Women's Day, and Celebration of Life. Let us strive for peace.

The Royal Princess

You are a princess,
Choosing the month and day when
You will greet the world,
Capturing the headlines in the media.
Your parents, the Duke and Duchess of Cambridge,
Proudly presented you to anxiously waiting people
Outside Saint Mary's Hospital.
The kind wishes of people waiting to celebrate
Your arrival and congratulating your parents
As you are the spare heir and fourth in line to the throne.
You were born in the morning at 8:34 on Saturday, May 2, 2015,
At Saint Mary's Hospital in the private Lindo Wing,
Where your father, your uncle Harry, and
your brother were also born.

Your anticipated arrival date was in April.
You decided to wait a little longer.
Perhaps you did not want to get wet
In the April showers.
To me it makes sense as girls are made of
Sugar and spice with a smile so nice.
May brings nature alive with flowers blooming,
Birds twittering, animals playing,
Scents of the flowers romanticizing the stage,
Sunshine with mild temperatures,
No umbrella to hold.
The people can wait until they are told
You have arrived. Then they can celebrate and cheer.
You have made news for this year.
May 2, 2015, is a date the world will remember.

The Duke and Duchess of Cambridge have
Formally registered your birth name as

FERIAL IMAM HAQUE

Princess Charlotte Elizabeth Diana.
Each name has deep symbolism.
Your maternal aunt Pippa's middle name is Charlotte.
It is also the feminine form of Charles,
Your paternal grandfather.
Your middle names Diana and Elizabeth
Pay tribute to the Queen your great-grandmother
And your late paternal grandmother.
You are bonded to your family members.
The name of each member is written by journalists and other writers,
Not only in the pages of British history
But also in the periodicals of other nations.

I am inspired by your chosen birthday.
May is important as we already
Celebrate Mother's Day on May 10 in Canada.
Then comes our national holiday, Victoria Day, and
The Tulip Festival with a rich royal Dutch history,
But it reminds me of cherishing the joys of motherhood.

Motherhood. Ferial with her baby.

Away from my birthplace in Chakma raja's residence
In a faraway country with British history
Now known as Bangladesh,
I waited alone patiently for my loving daughter
In the hospital bed with nobody to greet us.

The meaning of my name is "queen."
But I am just an ordinary person like the people
Patiently waiting for your arrival
In front of the steps of Saint Mary's Hospital.
You are the fourth in line to the throne.
Nobody worried about your gender.
Even if you have another brother,
Under the 2013 Succession to Crown Act,
You precede him as heir to the throne.
One retail expert has already predicted
You will be worth 150 million pounds
Annually, adding to the British economy,
Predominantly fueling the fashion and beauty industries.
You will be the talk of many people in many
Households in many countries.

When I was a little girl I dreamed
Of changing the world,
So I chose to be a chemist and scientist.
I persevered and achieved my goal.
But in my day women had very little scope
To continue to contribute
Until they retired.
So, like the other people in this world, I am
Wishing you all the power you have
To make the world a better place.
Now the world can celebrate

FERIAL IMAM HAQUE

November 10, 2017

Christmas 2016

My Memories

Christmas will soon be here,
A public holy holiday
Around the world to celebrate
The birth of a very special person
We all know as Jesus Christ.

The history of Christmas Day
Tells us Jesus was born in a manger
In Bethlehem on December 25, 1 BC.
His mother's name was Mary,
And his father was Joseph.

People from many corners of Jerusalem
Came to give Jesus their blessings.
The stars in the sky were shining bright,
Glittering like diamonds.

Today and almost seventy years ago
I would wonder how clever God was to
Light the sky up so high to welcome
Jesus Christ and announce his birth.

I remember when I was a child in London, England,
In 1950–1952, our class friends would
Tell us of their excitement about the Christmas celebration
After New Year's, when we were back at school.

They spoke of the gifts Santa brought for them and
Red Christmas stockings with white borders
Hanging on ledge of the mantel of the fireplace,
Which was packed with little toys and candies.

Of course, we all believed Santa traveled
In his sleigh with Rudolph the Reindeer
Whether there was fluffy white snow or not.
O what a wonderful time it must be!

At our school, Strand-on-the-Green,
I enjoyed choir practice under the direction of
Miss Davis and the pianist, Mrs. White,
For the Christmas concert before the Christmas holiday.
These memories again became alive
In the 1970s in Ottawa, Canada, when our children
Joined the school band, playing different instruments.

Now I became a participant, hosting
The special Christmas concert for all parents, children,
Relatives, and friends. Children sold the tickets
To family and friends to raise money for the choir.

Refreshments were served at intermission.
O what sweet memories of Christmas,
Both as a child and a mother.

In Canada, we celebrate the Christmas season
In December with friends and family,
Cooking special foods, attending concerts.
We love ballet and to dream of sugar plum fairies,
Mice, and soldiers dancing through the holiday season.
The Nutcracker ballet is an annual
Canadian Christmas tradition with performances
Wowing audiences from coast to coast.

The National Ballet of Canada's ballerinas
Have used 5,548 pairs of pointed shoes
For performances between 1995 and February 2011.
Just a little curious search on the internet gave me that information.
O imagine this statistical count!

Canada is a very large country with people from
Many corners of the world and different traditions
Influenced by their countries of origin, like France,
England, Ireland, Scotland, Germany, and Holland, plus the
First Nations. These and many more enrich our holiday.

We love to brighten the exteriors of our houses,
And our trees and shrubs, with Christmas lights.
Some like to have Santa in his sleigh with
Rudolph the Reindeer in the front on a snowy lawn.

We Canadians love an exotic Christmas menu:
Big Turkey, stuffing, potatoes (baked in foil or just baked and
Mashed), carrots, peas, brussels sprouts, sauerkraut,
Beets pickled or boiled, gravy. We enjoy egg nog.
It is very popular during the Christmas season.

Cakes and cookies fill the shelves of the stores:
Gingerbread men, fruitcake, shortbread.

Christmas tree in my home in Ottawa

We enjoy unwrapping gifts under the Christmas tree
Decorated with Christmas ornaments, candy canes,
Festive lights of many shapes and sizes, flowers, and fruits.
We enjoy cracking open Christmas crackers and unpacking stockings.
These are facts of the Canadian way of celebrating the holiday season.

Have a wonderful Christmas wherever you are!
Merry Christmas, and walk under the mistletoe.
Happy New Year 2017 to all from Canada.
We will be celebrating the 150th birthday of Canada.
You are all invited to Ottawa.

Christmas In Canada

I have lived in many countries where the Christmas holidays are celebrated different from Canada. Memories of Christmas in my childhood in London, England was not like the way the Canadians or Americans Celebrate. So, I wished to write how we celebrate Christmas in Canada for my sisters living in England.

In Canada, we celebrate Christmas from coast to coast with many different Christmas traditions. Canada is a very large country with people from many corners of the world. Many traditions are influenced by people's country of origin, such as France, England, Ireland, Scotland, Germany, and Holland, plus the First Nations.

Christmas in Canada is very different from Christmas in other countries like England, Bangladesh. Outside, the trees, bushes, evergreens, roads, sidewalks, driveways, and walkways are covered in white snow, giving everything a serene look. Inside the house we have warmth with the green Christmas tree beautifully decorated with ornaments, garlands, candy canes, and lights of many colors and shapes. Some houses have the fireplace decorated with Christmas stockings hanging for Santa Claus to drop in the gifts. We love to brighten the exteriors of houses, and the trees and shrubs, with Christmas lights. Some like to have Santa in his sleigh with Rudolph the Reindeer in the front on a lawn covered in snow.

The story of the television show *Rudolph the Red-Nosed Reindeer* is fascinating in that all the characters' voices (except for Sam the Snowman) were performed by Canadian actors, singers, and voice-over artists at the RCA Victor Studios in Toronto. In Canada, every year after 1964, the department stores have hosted an annual viewing of the "animagi" holiday special *Rudolph the Red-Nosed Reindeer.*

We Canadians love to visit the department stores to buy our gifts. To mention statistics, Canadian records show that total sales are nearly $3.2 billion. We love to pop the cork and raise a glass to welcome Christmas. We spend about $1.6 billion at Canada's beer, liquor, and wine stores for booze.

In 2005 residents of Alberta spent $967 on average per person in retail stores, more than any other Canadian province. Citizens of the Yukon and Northwest Territories spent $928 and $926 each, respectively.

Christmas dinner at my home

We Canadians love an exotic Christmas menu with a big turkey, stuffing, potatoes (baked in foil or just baked and mashed), carrots, peas, brussels sprouts, sauerkraut, beets (pickled or boiled), and gravy. Last year Canadians purchased a total of 3.9 million whole turkeys (report from Canadian farmers). So, there are a lot of drumsticks, wings, wishbones, sandwiches, and casseroles.

FERIAL IMAM HAQUE

Eggnog is popular during the Christmas season. According to statistics, Canadians consumed 5.8 million liters in December 2009. Gingerbread men, fruitcakes, shortbread cookies, candy canes, and festive lights are common. We enjoy unwrapping gifts under the Christmas tree and from the Christmas stockings. These surprising facts show the Canadian way of celebrating the holiday season.

We love Ballet to dream of Sugar Plum fairies, mice, and soldiers dancing through holiday season. The Nutcracker ballet is an annual Canadian Christmas tradition with performances wowing audiences from coast to coast. The National Ballet of Canada's ballerinas have used 5,548 pairs of pointed shoes for performances since 1995 to February 2011.

Canadians love Christmas Trees and we harvest about 5.5 million Christmas trees every year. Canada exported 2.25 million Christmas trees to over 25 countries including Japan, Mexico, the United States and Jamaica in 2006.

Christmas isn't only once a year but 365 days a year welcome at Reindeer Station (Northwest Territories), Christmas Island (Nova Scotia), Sled Lake (Saskatchewan), Holly (Ontario), Noel (Nova Scotia), Turkey Point (Ontario), and Snowflake (Manitoba). Since 1982, Santa's Post Office has employed mailroom elves from Canada, and he has received more than 20 million letters from children around the world. Canada Post volunteers donate over 200,000 hours of their time each year to help Santa respond to every letter that arrives on his doorstep.

Prelude to Chapter 10

In this chapter, the lives of women and their many roles are portrayed. But the primary role of women is expressed in the saying "The hand that rocks the cradle rules the world." In today's world perhaps, we are failing to teach morality to our children so that they may become good citizens.

Chapter 10

We Are Women

Because the people who are crazy enough to think they can change the world are the ones who do.

—Steve Jobs

Welcome, March 2015

I march along the snow-covered path, waiting eagerly to welcome the first day of spring on March 20, 2015. I did not realize this day was so special. We will be seeing a total solar eclipse in the final 29th degree of Pisces, bringing the month of March to a spectacular climax and initiating abundant opportunities.

March has occupied a soft corner in my heart since 1964. It was my first spring in Ottawa alone, and I was waiting to welcome motherhood, so far away from places where I grew up and was educated.

Ottawa then was not what it is today. My memories include experiences of growing up in two educational institutions and living in a small apartment with my husband. The most familiar and comforting places were the two libraries at Ottawa University and Carleton University.

Being able to speak the English language made me feel at home, but it was tough to translate scientific texts. With perseverance and endurance, I managed to learn about 50 percent of the jargon of science.

Anyway, coming back to my life where I had to cope with a multitude of responsibilities as a wife, mother, and student in a foreign land: it was tough. I grew up in a home where housekeepers and helpers performed the household chores. Today, while capturing my evaporating memories of half a century I can see the young me in my early twenties, so naive and tripping over small and big challenges. Yet I continued to keep walking toward my goalpost. My world was a child's world of fantasy and fairy tales.

March has been so special in my life. I celebrate the special days alone or with groups, my sisters, and/or my daughters. I see my efforts have morphed into beautiful crystalline forms of many shapes and sizes, sprinkled with rainbow colors.

On March 2, the Canadian Federation of the University Women (CFUW) of which I am a member, celebrated our eleventh year of International Women's Day with many activities and information

FERIAL IMAM HAQUE

on women's issues—health, rights, and education—along with food, presentations, and surprise door prizes.

I became inclined as an immigrant professional woman to retrace the history, anecdotes, of involvement of International Women's Week in Ottawa in 1976. I eagerly shared it with my two sisters living on the other coast of the Atlantic Ocean.

I wrote to my sister, saying, "How nice to read your email first thing in the morning on March 10, 2015, Commonwealth Day in Canada!" It has a deep meaning in my life. I came to Ottawa, Ontario, Canada, as the wife of a Commonwealth Scholar in 1963. Back then, marriage was more important than education for a young woman.

March is littered with important events, such as the following:

- Canadian Federation of University Women - Eleventh Anniversary of International Women's Week (March 2)
- International Women's Day (March 8) 2016, 2015
- Daylight saving time (begins March 9) 2014
- Commonwealth Day (Canada) (March 10) 2015,
- Pi Day, which recognizes the value of π (the Greek letter pi has great implication in mathematics) (March 14)
- Mother's Day in Britain (March 15) 2015
- St. Patrick's Day (March 17) 2014
- First day of spring (March 20) 2014, 2016
- Total solar eclipse (March 20)
- Daylight saving time in Britain (March 28) in 2015

So, I celebrate and observe these important days in the month of March.

Celebrating International
Women's Week 1976

The Ottawa Multicultural Women's Conference
Was sponsored by the Ministry of the Interior and received
Different levels of government funding,
Making it possible for it to be hosted at Skyline Hotel, Ottawa.
We celebrated International Women's Week 1976
To voice the concerns of new Canadians and immigrant women.

Each member of the Interim Organizing Committee
Had certain roles to play.
My responsibilities were
To write each member's bio
In addition to leading the workshop called
Immigrant Women in the Family.

I volunteered to host the dinner afterward
and provide musical entertainment,
Depicting an Indian Muslim wedding scene
\]With dance, song, and a bride dressed in a wedding dress.
It was eye-catching, and audiences were mesmerized.

I was invited to be part of a very powerful organization, the
Ottawa Folk Arts Council,
Responsible for hosting all the events and festivals in Ottawa such as
Canada's birthday celebration, the Tulip
Festival, and the summer festivals, and
Welcoming foreign dignitaries.
The most memorable one was when
Forty children and I dressed in ethnic costumes
And lined up along the corridor of the West Tower

FERIAL IMAM HAQUE

At Parliament Hill, Ottawa, Canada to welcome
Her Royal Highness Queen Elizabeth II and
Prince Philip
To Parliament Hill during their visit in 1979.

In 1976 for Canada's birthday I played a major role and
Organized an Indian dance by two little girls
On the main stage at Vincent Massey Park.
I wrote the dance theme in English and did the narration.
Members of the City Organizers become
Interested in Indian dance and music as a result.
I contacted friends who'd actively participated in the program.
The grant from the government was an incentive
To open dance and music schools,
And schools for Indian language and art
This is the history of how different cultural practices,
Flavors, and fine arts spread in Ottawa.

Recommendations from the conference
Have brought about a great change to the face of Ottawa.
We all enjoy the flavor and taste of multiculturalism today.
In Little Italy and Chinatown in the West End of Ottawa,
I was greeted with a special welcome
By local businesses and restaurants.

But I did want to continue with my research in chemistry.
The University of Ottawa's Chemistry Department
Opened the door for me to begin new research
In forensic science.
This how I became a forensic scientist.
The research publications
Introduced me to many research organizations
In many corners of the world.
I received letters from them asking for details

Of individual methods for
Updating the fingerprint development techniques
In the existing manuals.

The letters came from Turkey, Hawaii, Hong Kong,
the California State Police Department, the
FBI, and the
British Home Office.

What Fools We Were!

I am a woman and proud to be one.
Today, I am a scientist, a chemist, and more.
I am a survivor and seeker of knowledge.
I search for the truth and the true meaning of love.

Perhaps many great thinkers have
Written their thoughts on this topic.
A few of them are
Sir George Cockerill, Peter Harrington,
George R. R. Martin, and
Virginia Woolf, who wrote *A Society*.

"What fools we were!"
Has a deeper connotation than
I would have thought.
Have women left any deeper meaning
To set example for our world today?

Yes, women have paved the path for their rights.
The world celebrates their rights
On March 8, Women's Day.
Yet women celebrate around the world during
International Women's Week in March.

As a woman scientist, I know
We are all indebted to
One famous woman for her gift to
Humankind, the miracle of the x-ray.
The name Madame Curie will be remembered by men and women
For her sacrifice,
Along with that of her husband, Pierre Curie,
For having isolated the miracle radiant element radium.

My rights as a Canadian and a woman.
I turn back through the pages of the history of Canada
To learn of the dedication and courage of
Five Alberta women who fought for the rights
Of Canadian women to be recognized constitutionally.
As persons they are
Emily Murphy, who led the battle, and her supporters
Irene Parlby, Louise McKinney, Henrietta Muir Edward,
And Nellie McClung.
They came to be known as the "Famous Five."
October 18 is now known as Persons Day in Canada.

On the grounds of Parliament Hill in Ottawa, Ontario,
The monument created by Barbara Paterson
Was unveiled to memorialize the special event on October 18, 2000,
To commemorate the Persons case, and
The Famous Five women involved.

I found the true meaning of being a woman.
These are only a few of the women who have inspired me
To be a proud Canadian woman and work
For women's issues and my concerns,
Hoping every little portion of what I contribute will voice our
Need for girls and women in any walk of life
In the global society, both today and tomorrow.

We as women were not fools but pioneers.
Our contributions, however small they may be,
Have changed many facets of humanity.

What Mother Meant to Me

A mother has deep meaning in a child's heart.
I have the same reaction.
We all say, *I love you, Mother,* in our hearts,
But do we know what we mean?

On Mother's Day I write to express my emotions.
As a mother, I know what it feels like to be a mother.
We mothers rock the cradles and feed and nurture our children,
Hopefully to lead them to be good citizens.

I grew up under the umbrella of my dear mother.
It was many decades ago.
She worked under many trying circumstances,
As she was a widow in the early forties.
The societal setup was very unkind toward a widow so young.
She was blessed with three daughters
But had no son to carry the torch of the family!

Many a days in my mature age, I read her books.
My emotional reaction carries me to another world.
I wonder why a woman's social status changes overnight,
Why society imposes restrictions on a widow.

I happily grew up under your umbrella, Mother.
I was blessed with education, music, and housekeeping skills.
Of course, it became your responsibility to ensure that
As a parent you made the decision to hand over
Your daughters to eligible bachelors,
Each of who would lovingly care for his wife
As a responsible husband.

As a philosopher, administrator, and teacher,
You instilled good values in us and taught us to be ladies.

You taught me to live with my self-identity and dignity.
Soon it was time to leave the shade of your umbrella.

It was September 1963, just after my final
Honors exam in chemistry.
I departed to join my husband,
Whom I did not know well.
I can tell you, life was very different,
But I managed to survive.
I still value your teaching.
Education certainly shows the path

Mother and I in 1962 at her official residence,
Ruquayyah Hall, Dhaka University campus, East Pakistan

To
Self-identity for a woman to live in society
With independent respect.
Hopefully, I have met your expectations
As your daughter!

The last few years of your life when

FERIAL IMAM HAQUE

I was confined to bed with a mobility impairment,
We become bonded as two thinkers
Separated by the vast continents.
I personally came to see you
At your ninetieth birthday party in 2007!

You said goodbye to the world
On June 22, 2009.
You are now resting in peace in your final resting place,
Yet your memories are housed
In the museum and your praises
Sung in the auditorium.
Thank you for your dedicated sacrifice
For your three daughters.
We have grown up to be professional women
In the global community!

I want to conclude this chapter with a few words from Maya Angelou. She was a great soul to speak for black people and "visible" minority groups including women. I am touched by her words below, which express my feelings as a woman and visible minority:

"You alone are enough. There is nothing you have to prove to anybody."

Seniors Day in Canada

I am a senior living in
Canada's capital, Ottawa.
I am proud to be a Canadian
As I have grown up to be
Who I am today.

When I was in my thirties
In the seventies,
I remember many Canadians
Saying they had made Canada their home,
Having survived either World War I or World War II.
Others had escaped natural calamities.
And we can't forget those who knew the
Hunger pangs of the Potato Famine.

I did not know why Canadian seniors
Said of themselves that they were in their
Golden years.
Oh yes, there are a lot of senior discounts.
What else?
Searching for the golden rays?
They seemed nonexistent,
So I could not discover the point!

Canada is a country of immigrants
From many corners of the world
With diversity in their culture and their skills.
You could say that maybe they are
Trailblazers, role models, and survivors
Of Natural and man-made calamities,
Having come to Canada to find *a home* amid peaceful surroundings.

FERIAL IMAM HAQUE

Escaping the disasters of a war
For the birth of a new country,
I left my birth country, never to look back
But to search for a land in a new country
Where I could build a new home to raise my family,
To give them many opportunities in life.
I felt comfortable and at home in Ottawa
With people who'd had similar experiences,
So I, too, decided to make my home here almost four decades ago.

Now in my golden years,
I discover many bitter realities
Of day-to-day living with many struggles,
Yet I am not willing to give up and disappear
From the community I have been a part of.
In my younger days as a scientist and volunteer,
I drafted and published many papers to make our
Global community one of contentment and peace.

We, struggled, tripped, and worked tirelessly
To build the Canada we call our home.
Here we leave our dreams, our blueprints
To survive and thrive without any families.
We know the meaning of poverty, hunger pangs.
We have survived the blizzards and freezing rains,
Yet we are proud to be Canadians, to
Sing the songs of our successes and failures
Over the years in this land so artistically created,
The precious gift to us by our Creator.

Happy Seniors Day!

Prelude to Chapter 11

This chapter depicts the real world and the facts of life. It provides a snapshot of the joyous and sad occasions of life: birth, growth, and death. At the end of life, one leaves behind the legacy of one's good work. People are remembered only by their work and not for their wealth. On the headstones in the graveyards are inscribed the person's name and two important dates, the date of birth and the date of death, with a dash in between. The fact is, a life begins and sooner or later ends.

Chapter 11

Sad Occasions

Sadness flies away on the wings of time.

—Jean de la Fontaine

Red Poppy Day 2016

On Friday, November 11, 2016, in Canada
We will remember the brave Canadian soldiers
Who sacrificed their lives for Canada. This day marks
the anniversary of end of the World War I
hostilities on November 11, 1918.

Remembrance Day is also known as Armistice Day
or Poppy Day. The red color symbolizes the blood
Of the soldiers who died on the battlefield,
While white poppies campaigns are for nonmilitary
Interventions into the conflict situations.

In Canada, Friday, November 11, 2016, is
A special day to honor the brave soldiers
for their patriotism as Canadians who stood by our allies
To end the World War I hostilities with the
Germans on November 11, 1918,
To bring Peace to the world!

Before November 11, many people wear
Red poppies to remember the fallen soldiers.
White poppies signify the loss of nonmilitary civilians.
There are great emotional scars among servicemen
And communities whose sons, brothers, fathers, uncles,
And grandfathers lost their lives.

The practice of wearing of a poppy as a symbol of remembrance
Originates from a poem penned by John McCrea,
A Canadian doctor serving in the military.
In the world's most well-known war poem, "In Flanders Fields,"
McCrea highlights the red poppies growing in the
Flemish graveyards where soldiers were buried.

McCrea, after the burial of his close friend and a former student,
Alexis Helmer, killed by a German shell at the battlefront on
May 3, 1915 during the second battle of Ypres, Belgium,

Wrote the words of the first stanza. These words touch my heart
As I remember leaving the war zone
In my birth country and migrating to Canada to make it my home.

"In Flanders Fields the poppies blow
Between the crosses, row on row,
That mark our place: and in the sky
The larks still bravely singing fly
Scarce heard amid the guns below."

In Ottawa at the National War Memorial,
Official national ceremonies are held to a strict protocol.
On November 11, organized church services
Include playing of the "Last Post,"
A reading of the fourth verse of the
"Ode of Remembrance," and
Two minutes' silence at 11:00 a.m.

Then there is the laying of wreaths on the War Memorial
By armed forces and many dignitaries and
Community groups. Following is a presentation by military officials.
This marks the anniversary of end of the World War I
Hostilities on November 11, 1918.

In May 2000, in a special ceremony, the
Remains of an unidentified Canadian soldier
Who died in France in World War I were laid
In the Tomb of the Unknown Soldier
At the National War Memorial.
Since then members of the public have laid
Poppies, letters, and pictures
at the National War Memorial in Ottawa, Ontario, Canada.

Similar services are held across the country.
Some schools are open on this day to hold
Special assemblies, lessons, and presentations
On armed conflicts and those who gave their lives.

FERIAL IMAM HAQUE

Farewell

Nobody knows my pain.
All my work has been done in vain.
"Oh no!" I say. "Let us find a way
To take a big stride and walk away."

Let's bid farewell to old days and
Dream of creative ways
For tomorrow and the day after.
Hope for brighter days full of laughter.

Think of days in the spring when
Birds are perched on trees singing and
The sun is shining on the flowers,
Waiting for a spring shower.

Soon the warmth of the summer sun
Will enhance the budding flowers, which will
Grow into tasty fruits and vegetables.
We will enjoy our meals with this delicious menu
For the rest of the year amid sunshine, rain, or snow,
Thanks to my dream!

Memories of Jean Pigott

Wednesday morning, I picked up the *Ottawa Sun* from my mailbox. The front page shocked me. I remained still for a while, unable to believe what I was reading:

Jean Pigott

1924–2012

Political pioneer, remembered as passionate
community leader, booster for the capital.

My fingers turned to page 3 to find in boldface: "Farewell, Queen Jean."

As Susan Sherring, *Ottawa Sun* correspondent, writes, "Visionary, political pioneer, cookie lady, Pigott always put others first."

Inside, the article read, "As city mourns, family remembers a mother, grandmother, and role model. Pigott died on Tuesday morning, leaving her family and friends in sadness, and taking with her 87 years' worth of personal memories of city history."

Although, I had not met Jean Pigott personally, I did have the pleasure of corresponding with her on two important matters concerning community history of the City of Ottawa in 1986: Winterlude in 1986, and then again in 1989 on the topic of "Safety of Students: Traffic Lights on Brookfield Road, and Near All Educational Institutions." Back then I was president of the Brookfield High School Parents' Association and chair of the Teacher–Parent Advisory Committee of Brookfield High School, Ottawa Board of Education.

Yes, we did receive the support we needed to reach our goal. The traffic lights were turned on, on Brookfield Road and the intersections of McCarthy Road and Plant Drive, McCarthy and Paul Anka, and Ridgemont and Altavista Drive, to name a few

We did not neglect the two universities, Ottawa and Carleton Universities.

FERIAL IMAM HAQUE

I remembered the book *The Dash* by Linda Ellis and Mac Anderson. Jean Pigott's Dash definitely brought many changes to the city of Ottawa over the years.

In 2011, I had the pleasure of meeting her sister, Grete Hale, and Gay Cook at a community event at Hunt Club Riverside Community Centre. I could not resist buying her book entitled *The Baker's Daughter*.

I had the honor of attending the convocation in 2009 at Carleton University, when Grete was awarded an honorary doctoral degree for her contributions to the community.

Grete and I had a little chat about our writing interests and community work to change the city of Ottawa.

All I could do was to send Jean's family a sympathy card to her address in Bayne House. The front cover of the card read as follows:

In
memory
and in
celebration
of someone who made
this world
a
brighter
and
better place.

Inside it read as follows:

With
Deepest Sympathy

Sincerely,

Ferial Haque, PhD
January 12, 2012
Ottawa

Remembrance Day of Death

The Remembrance Day of Death
Has always baffled me as long as
I can remember
Because I missed my dear father!

I realized as I grew up to become a woman that
Every creature, small or big, in this world that is
Born and celebrates birthdays
Will leave their near and dear ones one day,
Saying
Goodbye for eternity.

Today, June 22, 2018, is one of those days.
I sit and relax to scan my memories of yesterday.
Like recording the infrared or Nuclear Magnetic Resonance (NMR)
Spectroscopy of a compound, I see
Random lines floating in my imagination, so clear.

It has been a long time—more than half a century—since
I came to Ottawa and entered a small apartment.
It felt like being enclosed in a secure cube, a cage.
There was a telephone on the dresser with a
number, a receiver, and a ringer.

Now, I travel back to my memory land to discover I was alone!
I can hear those voices echoing, "She is like an orphan.
Alone, confined in a cube, like a caged bird with no wings!'
Yet no one knew my dreams of creating a new me.

I missed my father and my mother. Sometimes my tears
Poured like the raindrops, washing away my wishful dreams.
Living and growing up in the warmth of my childhood home, I had
Many sweet dreams, memories, and creative ideas for my future.

FERIAL IMAM HAQUE

Today, my identity is that of a professional scientist, wife, and mother.
Standing alone in my new country with many diverse identities,
I live in my home with little spare time left to regret sadness,
Accepting that everyone will say goodbye, including my mother.

Reversing the memory clock, I count nine years. I stop to think.
Like a child I was crying because Mother took her last breath.
Indeed, she was pronounced dead in my birthland so far away.
Helplessly wiping my tears, I was alone,
gazing at my computer screen.

Wherever I went, all I could tell people was "My mother is dead,"
I pulled out a Kleenex and with a tender touch wiped my tears.
Alone, each day I grew stronger as memories of Mother faded.
Now, I look out through the patio door and the bay window.

Time, which equals life, is the healer of both
emotional and physical wounds.
During the past nine years, I have been burdened with duties
I didn't know how to do or even what to
do! I wish I knew where to go
To get a few pointers to complete these unwanted tasks.

Under such unwanted burden and threats I lost control and fell
In the parking lot at the shopping mall last year.
I have been recovering alone, again looking through my patio door
And the bay window like the caged bird singing my song,
Hoping for the freedom to take a deep breath of the fresh air.

Life Ends

Sooner or later
Life will end.
Those who care
Come to hear
The funeral service
And join in the prayer to praise.

The final act will be
To lay the coffin in the final resting place.
On the tombstone will be engraved
Two very important dates
With a dash in between,
The year of birth and the year of death.

Those who care to remember
Why and how each day was spent
Will sing in praise of the good deeds.
Everyone will remember
To sing in praise and cheer.

This is how life ends,
But good works remain
Alive and fresh among family and friends.
We filter only works done and cheer.

FERIAL IMAM HAQUE

February 7, 2018

Final Words

Life begins with a cry when a child arrives to join us in the worldly setting. Our children grow under the care of their parents to be good citizens of the global community. We age and become a symbol of praise, respect, and admiration, on the positive stratum of society. But we can't forget the negative stratum—to become an outcast. In our senior years we are unwelcome in society as we slow down and become less productive. Moreover, we require care and support from the people around us.

Why? I can't say. But while I was a child in school in East Pakistan, one song, composed by the Nobel Laurate poet Rabindranath Tagore, from his book *Gitanjali*, was my motivator, as it remains even today. My English translation of this is as follows:

> If nobody responds to your earnest call,
> Just move on and keep walking all alone
> On the path you have chosen for your life.
> Even if nobody acknowledges you,
> Keep walking and do not look back.

This song touched my heart, and the words are ingrained in my mind even now. This could be one reason why I wanted to create my own identity and be independent as I grew up. I was convinced that education was the only key to succeed. Yes, I was determined to acquire my PhD degree in chemistry, and I succeeded to achieve my goal in 1970, when I graduated from Strathclyde University, Glasgow, Scotland. The campus is situated close by the River Clyde, where the story of Bonnie and Clyde originated.

With time I was convinced that I was a very special little girl, so I needed to have great faith in myself and continue to fulfill my dreams, guided by my intuitive feelings.

Now, after almost seven decades, I console myself by saying I am following the the footsteps of my father and his legacy. Maybe because Father said goodbye to us at a premature age of twenty-seven years. I wanted to contribute the scientific to find cures for patients suffering from chronic pain. My father suffered from heart disease since his childhood. He had great faith in his loving wife to take on the responsibility of bringing up their three daughters to become responsible citizens of the global community. His wishes came true, and Mother did instill her ideology in her three daughters.

People in her society did remind her: "What will be the fate of your three daughters?! They are not beautiful like you. On the contrary, they are like their father. Moreover, they do not have a father or even a brother!"

These cruel words of people in society did have a great impact on my individuality. For better or for worse, I am a scientist. My scientific contributions can be found listed on the internet. My contributions as an activist in the community are found in the community and among political society. These are my final words about a little loving daughter of a favorite student of the physicist Professor S. N. Bose. Professor Bose has left his legacy—a famous legacy: the Bose–Einstein theory.

———————

As Wikipedia states, *Gitanjali* (Bengali: গীতাঞ্জলি, lit. *song offering*) is a collection of poems by the Bengali poet Rabindranath Tagore. Tagore received the Nobel Prize for Literature, largely for the book. It is part of the collection of the UNESCO Representative Works.

The original Bengali collection of 103–157 poems was published on August 14, 1910. The English *Gitanjali* or *Song Offerings* is a collection of 103 English poems of Tagore's own English translations of his Bengali poems first published in November 1912 by the India Society of London.

February 21, 2018

The Pink Peonies

I have chosen pink peonies as a symbol of my success.

- The pink color symbolizes the pink sari I wore for my convocation ceremony to receive my PhD degree diploma with honors.
- I blossomed like a flower amid the many painful setbacks during this journey.

Pink peonies were grown in my backyard garden. The story of how I got the peony bulbs intrigues me even today. Gardening has been my hobby since childhood. I am fascinated with pale-colored flowers in the garden.

When the peonies are in full bloom along the fence in my backyard, it reminds me of how I got the bulbs in the early eighties. I was planning for designing the garden, both a flower and vegetable garden.

My husband, I and our younger daughter had a favorite nursery in Ottawa from where we used to buy all our gardening supplies. One day, we went to buy some seeds and seedlings for the garden. Looking around the indoor displays, we were tired. So, we went to look at the outdoor displays. It was difficult to decide what we wanted for the garden. I sat on a chair to talk it over with my husband.

I found some bulbs in a wheelbarrow nearby. I felt that if I could have those at a reduced price, I would be able to plant them in the garden and take care to get the best flower. My husband and I talked about the idea of asking the person working in the garden if I could buy them at a reduced price. Of course, we did not know what the color of the flowers would be. We had already bought bulbs from indoor displays.

Anyway, I decided to ask the person working in the garden. To my surprise, I was told I could have them for free. We selected some healthy bulbs and then finished our shopping and went home.

After lunch, I planted the bulbs along the bay window with the other bulbs. We lovingly nurtured the bulbs, and in time the plants were loaded with amazingly beautiful pink flowers! The neighbors would stop and admire the pink peonies:

The joy of seeing the pink peonies gave me feeling of great success, self-confidence, and admiration for my past personal achievements to dream of a new venture to solve new problems in science and society.

Since my last contract on forensic science, I focused on creating my own way of earning money to manage the household expenses.

My house was the place where I wrote the manuscripts of my research findings in forensic science for publication in international journals and Canadian police magazines in forensic science in the eighties. I diligently worked away as if I were in the chemistry laboratory. I wanted my place of work to be neat and tidy and to have a beautiful garden. I did achieve my goal to publish with the groups where I began the project. Of course, my house was my official point of contact. I did receive letters of inquiry and requests for information as a research scientist in Ottawa. Requests for information on the technical aspects came from different research groups in many countries.

The request came from the community to write about my experiences as a scientist and immigrant, juggling the many roles of wife and mother. Then it was difficult to fund the project and find a mentor to guide me through to complete this idea.

So, I decided to enroll in writing courses in Ottawa and take correspondence courses from the United States to obtain a diploma. I did this while keeping myself active with political issues relevant to women, children, the education system, and multiculturalism in Ottawa.

I started dreaming of my life as a teenager, when I thought of becoming a scientist. I'd been able to realize that dream. I have studied and trained at many universities in different countries on different continents.

It all began in 1960 when I enrolled in the Department of Chemistry, University of Dhaka, East Pakistan, in the three-year honors program in chemistry. I was the only female student in the program. My expenses for the program were paid by the Governor General's Scholarship.

I also won the Governor General's Award for outstanding academic performance in high school.

I felt honored and proud of myself because my father was an outstanding student and had graduated from the Department of Physics in the same university. He obtained an honors degree in 1935 and an MSc degree in 1936. Father was one of the favorite students of Professor S. N. Bose of Bose–Einstein theory fame (*Our Alma Mater*, Dhaka Physics Group).

According to my family tradition, I accepted the vow of marriage in 1962. After that I was faced with many challenges in life. Having completed my honors degree, I moved forward to join my husband, who was a graduate student studying for his PhD in the Department of Chemistry, University of Ottawa, Canada.

This led me to begin my venture into many roles: wife, mother, and graduate student in a foreign land, battling to overcome the extreme winter in Ottawa. So many responsibilities would be daunting and overwhelming for anyone as young as I or even older than I. Sadly, at that time, there were no families from the Indian subcontinent, so I could not turn to anyone for support to help me settle into my new roles as a wife and mother.

I did not shy away from any of my roles in life that were thrust upon me. It was a long and lonely journey, but I accepted that it was the beginning of my personal learning and growth. I certainly was not going to be defeated by these multiple challenges, so I persevered, tirelessly tripping over many hurdles along the way.

Once again, I am dreaming away to narrate the other setbacks and unwanted experiences on my way to getting to where I am today. I discovered that people are people. Some gave me a feeling and sense of security to continue with my journey as a senior citizen.

This is the conclusion of this memoir, which is only a segment of my memories of growing up in Ottawa in the sixties in my early twenties.

These flowers are from my garden.

Epilogue

February 3, 2018

The time has come to end one phase of the story of my life. It has been a long and tiring journey since I landed at the small domestic Ottawa airport in 1963. As a new bride not knowing my husband well, I dreamed of our honeymoon in a faraway land—Ottawa, Canada's capital. It was not what I had expected. Time has gone by so fast. I pause to count how long. Well, I can only count decades and not years in order to make it simple. More than half a century has elapsed since I discovered my identity amid the Canadian multicultural mosaic in the seventies.

My sincere endeavor to raise our two daughters has not been smooth sailing given that I was a professional woman and immigrant, having survived the battlefield of the Dhaka University campus, Dhaka, Bangladesh.

My slogan for women's dignity and self-identity is that women should receive an education to acquire knowledge in many areas of life in order to be self-sufficient.

The past decade has not been easy with my husband's progressive disease. I have no alternative but to accept the reality of being separated from him because of this unavoidable circumstance. As a senior, my life has its limitations. I am still residing in my home on Lillico Drive, Ottawa.

February 3, 2018

Afterword

My Chosen Words came into being when the dream of the author was shattered into a million pieces almost thirty-five years ago in Ottawa, Canada. She was bewildered by the actions and comments of her maternal family and her husband, depicting the culture of the country where women literally have no independent existence, visibility, or say. Unable to accept their proposition, her focus was steered to how she could embark on her role as a scientist.

The author's dream as a professional scientist was put on hold to investigate the personalities and abilities of immigrants unfamiliar with the culture and setting of a pioneering professional scientist. She began her journey in Ottawa as the only female graduate student in chemistry going back more than half a century.

People around her probably wondered, *How can a woman from a developing country dressed in a sari, with a different culture and language, fit into the male-oriented society of Canada?* These were possibly the whispers among her male peers more than fifty years ago.

Yet she continued to learn and walk on her chosen path to complete all the formalities for her PhD degree. Her determination paid off. She was awarded the PhD degree at the Summer Convocation at Strathclyde University, Glasgow, Scotland, in 1970. When she came to Ottawa, she availed herself of every opportunity to teach and continue her research.

She failed to accept the role of a woman as a wife and mother. Therefore, she was an outcast in society. And because she was not the mother of a son, she was looked down upon.

She continued to establish her identity as a scientist and mother, voicing the rights of women to have their own identity and striving for *peace* globally.

Acknowledgments

The author sincerely thanks her younger sister Late Mrs. Shahwar Sadeque for encouraging her to complete *My Chosen Words*. Inspired by the last words of her beloved mother, Professor Akhtar Imam, the author embarked on the project.

Living in Ottawa for more than half a century, she provides a few answers to satisfy questions asked by curious students, colleagues, and others in the universities and government laboratories. In the earlier stages of her life she had to satisfy the curiosity of her two daughters when they were children.

Thank you all for motivating me to compile my answers, along with anecdotes and stories, in *My Chosen Words*.

My sincere thanks to the photographers who captured the images of people and places included in *My Chosen Words*. Sad but true, some of them are no longer with us. Their works have been preserved in my albums. These albums have traveled with me to many countries, including the battlefield of the Dhaka University campus during the liberation of Bangladesh on December 16, 1971. However, some of the photos I have taken myself in recent years.

Thank you all for enabling me to recollect my memories of many decades in order to depict the lives of my family in the twentieth and twenty-first centuries. Thanks to my younger sister Late Mrs. Shahwar Sadeque for providing me with a few pictures included herein.

Suggested Reading

Introduction

1. Robin Roberts. *From the Heart: Seven Rules to Live By.* New York: Hyperion, 2007.
2. Sandra Lee. *Made from Scratch: A Memoir.* Des Moines: Meredith Books, 2007.

Chapter 1

1. Akhtar Imam. My Life. Edited by Mohsin Shastrapani. Translated from Bengali by Enamul Haq. Revised by Pharhad Sadeque. Dhaka: Shaven Mahal, 2003. The Bengali edition, edited by Amar Ziban Katha (1917–1950), was published in July 1993.

Chapter 2

1. Peter L. Pauson. *Organometallic Chemistry.* London: Edward Arnold, 1967.
2. Ferial Haque. *The Influence of Iron and Manganese Carbonyls on the Reactivity of Cyclic Seven-Membered Organic Ligands.* Doctoral thesis, University of Strathclyde, Glasgow, June 1970.

Chapter 6

1. Maya Angelou. *The Complete Poetry*. New York: Random House, 2015.
2. Maya Angelou. *Rainbow in the Cloud: The Wisdom and Spirit of Maya Angelou*. New York: Random House, 2014.

Chapter 7

1. Parita Mukta. *Shards of Memory: Woven Lives in Four Generations*. London: Weidenfeld & Nicholson, 2002.
   Adrienne Clarkson. *Heart Matters*. Viking Canada, 2006.
2. Blanche Black. *Beyond Declining Years: The Art of Aging*. Penombra Press, 2002.
3. Eda Van der Linden. *They Ventured Forth! Stories of Dutch Canadians Who Settled in Osgoode Township, Ontario, 1940s–1960s*. Ottawa: Eda Van der Linden, 2010.
4. Grete Hale. *The Baker's Daughter: The Story of a Long, Rich, and very Canadian Life*. Ottawa: Ottawa Citizen, 2011.

Chapter 11

1. Dhaka Physics Group. *Our Alma Mater*. Elizabeth City, NJ: Mrs. Jutta Choudhury, Mrs. Anjuman-ara Rashid, and Mrs. Nazma Habib, 2006.

Bibliography

Angelou, Maya. Rainbow in the Cloud, The Wisdom and Spirit of ... New York: Random House, 2014.

Athill, Diana. *Somewhere towards the End.* London: Granata Publications, 2008.

Baldwin, Beulah. *The Long Trail: The Story of a Pioneer Family.* Edmonton, Alberta: NeWest Press, 1992.

Black, Blanche. *Beyond Declining Years: The Art of Aging.* Penumbra Press: Newcastle, Ontario, 2001.

Clarkson, Adrienne. *Heart Matters.: New York* Viking Canada, 2006.

Hale, Grete. *The Baker's Daughter: The Story of a Long, Rich, and Very Canadian Life.* Ottawa: The Ottawa Citizen, 2011.

Higham, Robin. *Who Do We Think We Are? Canada's Reasonable (and Less Reasonable) Accommodation Debates.* Ottawa: Invenire Books, 2009.

Hook, Edna Loveless. *Sir William Dawson and Henry Marshall Tory: The Achievements and Ideological Attitudes of Two Great Canadian Educators.* Ottawa: Carleton University, 1990.

Imam, Akhtar. *My Life.* Edited by Mohsin Shastrapani. Translated from Bengali by Enamul Haq. Revised by Pharhad Sadeque. Dhaka: Shafeni Mahal, 2003.

Jaffe, Bernard. *Crucibles: The Story of Chemistry, from Ancient Alchemy to Nuclear Fission.* 4th rev. ed. New York: Dover Publications, 1976.

James, P. D. A. *Certain Justice: Vintage Canada a Division of Randam House Canada Limited, 1997.*

James, P.D. *Time to Be in Earnest.: Autobiography Vintage Canada a Division of Randam House Canada limited, 2001.*

Latta, Ruth. *Life Writing: Autobiographers and Their Craft.* Burstows: General Store Publishing, 1988.

Lee, Sandra. *Made from Scratch. A Memoir: Iowa: Meredith Books, 2007.*

Mukta, Parita. *Shards of Memory: Woven Lives in Four Generations.* London: Weidenfeld & Nicholson, 2002.

Pannell, Chris, ed.. *Selections from New Writers Workshop: Between a Dock and High Place.* Hamilton, OH: Jasper Press, 1997.

Pauson, Peter L. *Organometallic Chemistry.* London: Edward Arnold, 1967.

Scruggs, Afi-Odelia. *Beyond Stitch and Bitch: Reflections on Knitting and Life.* Hillsboro, OR: Beyond Words, 2004

Van der Linden, Eda. *They Ventured Forth! Stories of Dutch Canadians Who Settled in Osgoode Township, Ontario, 1940s–1960s.* Ottawa: Eda Van der Linden, 2010.

FERIAL IMAM HAQUE

Index of Poem Titles

About the Author

Ferial Imam Haque is a retired scientist who lives in Ottawa. She has traveled to many countries since her early childhood. She has rich and diverse experiences, specializing in science and society. Through her powerful experiences she has contributed not only to the scientific community but also to the well-being of women and children.

Her conviction is that women are people and should have their individual identities, which can be achieved through education.

She was born to parents who were educated in the nineteen thirties in British India. Her father was a physicist, and her mother was a philosopher. She was awarded her PhD degree in chemistry by the University of Strathclyde, Glasgow, Scotland, in the Summer Convocation of 1970.

She emigrated to Ottawa, Canada, on July 1972, having survived the liberation movement of Bangladesh. It was a rough journey to prove her identity as a scientist and forensic scientist. She is dedicated to living in harmony in a society of diverse people and seeking to achieve a common understanding to appreciate and accept the many ethnicities of the people of Canada.

Her objective is to continue to document her rich international experiences in education and diversity as a senior citizen and a woman in the twenty-first century.

Ferial Imam is the daughter of remarkable parents who were both educationist in British India. She grew up and spent her life in the public eye at home and abroad. She has traveled and lived in many countries as a student and researcher. People around her have observed and shared her successes and hard times.

Hers is a story of triumph and turmoil while traveling through the many phases of her life: childhood, married life, maturity, depicting her vision as a daughter, sister, wife, student, scientist, and mother. She offers touching impressions of emigrating to Canada, leaving behind the tragedies of the battlefield. Beginning a new life as an immigrant professional woman in 1972 with sad memories was a challenge in Ottawa. It was not easy.

Her key role as a professional immigrant woman in the seventies was to savor some of the taste and flavor of multiculturalism in Ottawa, Canada's capital. Being a member of many groups in Ottawa, Ferial has introduced and implemented a new vision of who women are. With diversity and tolerance, she welcomes new Canadians from many corners of the world.

About the Book

My Chosen Words is the author's honest confession of how she persisted to rise above poverty, hunger, and isolation as a professional immigrant woman. Even in the darkest days of her life, she could see the sun rise. Her conviction and her devotion to research enabled her to contribute to the scientific world.

This powerful, emotional, and astonishing story will touch the hearts of women, immigrants, and young women pursuing higher studies and research in science. Ferial's personal narrative depicts how she overcame adversity to emerge from a dead end and find creative ways to develop her identity as a Canadian and secure a place in the global society.

She tumbled over many hurdles in her twenties, juggling her role as a wife, mother, and graduate student in the early sixties in Canada.